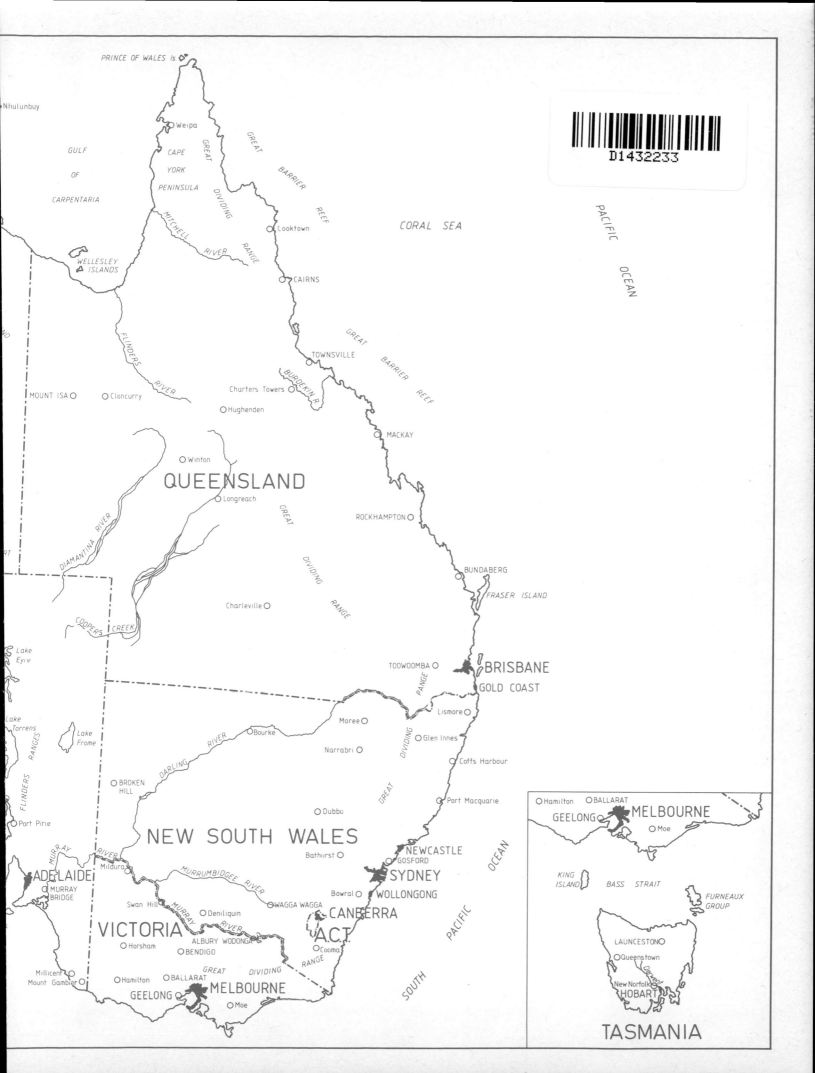

To MARCE

WITH OUR LOVE &
BEST WISHES. HAPPY TRAVELLING
LOVE FROM NAN & ALAN.

PRESENTING
AUSTRALIA

PRESENTING
AUSTRALIA

Text by Dalys Newman
Photographs by Bill Andrews, Trevern Dawes, Les Green,
Geoff Higgins, Peter Solness, Ian Wigney and others

NATIONAL
BOOK DISTRIBUTORS AND PUBLISHERS

Published by National Book Distributors and Publishers
3/2 Aquatic Drive, Frenchs Forest, NSW 2086, Australia

First edition 1981
Reprinted 1983, 1984
Second edition 1985
Reprinted 1986, 1987
Third edition 1989
Reprinted 1991, 1993, 1994

© Copyright: Text and Maps National Book Distributors and Publishers: 1981,
1985, 1989, 1994
© Photographs: Bill Andrews, Trevern Dawes, Les Green,
Geoff Higgins, Peter Solness, Ian Wigney, Ken Stepnell 1981, 1985, 1989, 1994
Typeset in Australia by Deblaere Typesetting Pty Ltd
Printed in Hong Kong by Everbest Printing Co. Ltd
National Library of Australia Cataloguing-in-Publication data

Newman, Dalys
Presenting Australia
ISBN 1 875580 14 X

1. Australia—Description and travel—1976–1990-Views.
2. Australia—Social life and customs—1976–1990—
Pictorial works. I. Andrews, Bill, 1924–   . II. Title.

994.0630222

Contents

Australia – Two Centuries

Australia – Two Centuries

AUSTRALIA, the world's smallest continent and largest island, is a land of contrast and contradiction. With shores washed by three oceans and four seas and an area of nearly 800 million hectares the diversity of scenery, climate and conformation is vast.

The breathtaking monotony of the barren red heartland is offset by iced peaks of snow in the mountains of the south-east, golden glowing pinnacles of the Macdonnell Ranges in the Northern Territory and behemoth sandstone monoliths such as Ayers Rock and the Olgas. Lush, steamy jungle and conifer dominated forest contrast with deserts of drifting sand dunes, large expanses of salt pan, dry creek beds and undulating savannah. There is no such thing as a typical Australian landscape and every Australian has his own interpretation of his country.

The Beginnings

Australia was the last great habitable land mass on earth to be surveyed and colonized by Europeans. Aeons before the explorers made their landfall, the Aborigines took possession of the vast, empty continent. They are believed to have travelled from Asia along transitory land bridges created by the rising and ebbing seas of the Ice Age. For thousands of years they occupied the continent undisturbed and undiscovered.

Myth, legend and vague map sketches indicate an awareness of *Terra Australis*, the Great South Land, during the centuries it remained uncharted. Inca, Greek and ancient Egyptian legend all speak of a great land to the south. Second-century geographers make reference to the land and in the Middle Ages it was sketched vaguely on the map. Japanese, Indonesian and Chinese mariners may have landed on its northern shores before the arrival of the first Europeans, but there is no incontrovertible evidence of this. It must be assumed

The Duyfken *in the Gulf of Carpentaria*

that the Portuguese were the first civilized men to sight the continent that was for centuries regarded as desolate and inhospitable. Although there is no documentary proof that the Portuguese ships sighted Australia, there is evidence that supports the possibility that these great seafarers exploring the archipelagos of the East Indies came within sight of the Australian coast before 1542.

In 1606, Torres, the Spaniard, sailed through the passage separating New Guinea from Australia, but probably missed sighting the southern continent. In the same year, the Dutch East India

8

Company ship, the *Duyfken,* under command of Willem Jansz, sailed down the west coast of Cape York Peninsula and the honour of the first recorded sighting of the continent by Europeans went to the Dutch. Jansz' reports spoke of a barren country inhabited by 'wild, cruel black savages'

Others followed. In 1696 Willem de Vlamingh reached the coast of Rottnest Island opposite modern Fremantle and named the Swan River after the black swans seen in abundance. Only one Englishman is known to have visited these shores before Captain Cook. This was William Dampier,

Natives opposing Captain Cook's Landing

and for ten years the Dutch kept well away from this area.

The next part of Australia to be filled in on the map was the west coast when the Dutchman Dirk Hartog made landfall about 720 km north of Perth in 1616. During the next 20 years Dutch navigators slowly filled in the gaps on the western and northern parts of the map.

In 1642, Abel Tasman, in his ship *Zeehaen,* skirted Tasmania, naming it Van Diemen's Land after Anthony Van Diemen, Governor General of the Dutch East Indies. His reports of this island were somewhat terrifying: he noted that several large trees had steps about 2 metres apart cut into their trunks, from which he deduced that the inhabitants must be a race of giants.

a navigator and pirate famous for his travels and writings. In 1688, his ship, the *Cygnet,* was driven far south by a typhoon and reached the north-west coast of Australia, near the present Buccaneer Archipelago. His first impressions of the country were bleak: 'The Land is of a dry sandy soil, destitute of water . . . the inhabitants of this Country are the Miserablest People in the world.'

He left unimpressed, but returned again in 1699 and anchored the *Roebuck* near Hartog's original landfall. His second impressions were no better

The First Fleet entering Botany Bay

Captain Phillip's first sight of Port Jackson

than his first. He remarked that except for the pleasure of discovering the most barren spot on the face of the globe, this coast of New Holland would not have charmed him much. His report effectively killed all interest in New Holland. It was the country that nobody wanted and for 70 years it was to remain unsought and virtually unseen.

Captain James Cook finally put Australia on the map. He discovered and charted the east coast and so paved the way for British settlement.

In 1768 Cook set out from England in the *Endeavour* to make astronomical observations in the Pacific. His secondary mission was to ascertain something more about the little known Australian continent. After completing his primary mission of observing the 1769 transit of Venus, Cook sailed southward, circumnavigated New Zealand and then determined to 'steer to the westward until we fall in with the east coast of New Holland'. On 19 April 1770, Cook sighted the east coast of New Holland. 'I have named it Point Hicks... the seashore is all white sand,' he wrote. It is now generally agreed that the spot he called Point Hicks is identical with the present Cape Everard, Victoria.

The ship anchored in Botany Bay on 29 April. The party went ashore to be met by defiant natives who dispersed only when one of their numbers was hit in the legs by a charge of small shot. After eight days of collecting specimens, drawing and noting trees, flowers and wildlife, the expedition sailed northward. Cook described the coast as 'diversified with an agreeable variety of hills, ridges, valleys and large plains'. Botanist, Joseph Banks declared that it had 'a great show of fertility'.

Cook sailed up the coast, naming the various bays and headlands as he passed. Occasionally he cast anchor and the voyagers went ashore to make acquaintance with kangaroos, dingoes, myriads of birds, snakes and the countless insect life of Australia.

He continued north, rounded Cape York and here, on a little island about 2 kilometres from the Cape he landed, hoisted the Union Jack and took formal possession of the whole of the eastern coast in the name of King George III. He called it New

10

South Wales. Although Cook's discovery aroused much interest, it was not until after Britain lost the war of Independence and hence her American Territories that colonization began.

During much of the eighteenth century criminals from Britain's overflowing gaols were sent to the American colonies. With the rebel colonists' victory in 1783 this outlet was suddenly and permanently closed. So, in 1787, the First Fleet under Captain Arthur Phillip set off for Botany Bay to establish a penal settlement. Finding Botany Bay inadequate for his purposes, Phillip sailed up to Port Jackson. Two days were spent examining the coves and bays until eventually Phillip found the perfect site for settlement. He named his encampment Sydney, after Lord Sydney, the Home Secretary. On 26 January 1788 Phillip raised the Union Jack and proclaimed

will not only occupy and rule this great country, but will also be the beneficent patroness of the entire southern hemisphere. How grand is the prospect which lies before the youthful nation!

Work began in earnest. Under command of the military the convicts began the formidable task of founding a settlement. Tents were erected and simple bark and thatching shelters constructed. It was soon evident that skilled tradesmen were few and far between, most of the convicts were not used to working on the land and tools were inadequate. Crops failed and the majority of the Government cattle breeding stock died. The people were poorly clothed, hungry and of low morale.

There was a great deal of drunkenness, and thieving — particularly of food — was rife. Food

Sydney Cove, August 1788, seven months after the arrival of the First Fleet

British sovereignty over the whole eastern half of the continent. The livestock was landed, and on 6 February, when the settlement began to look a little more comfortable, the women were brought ashore.

On the following day the Governor's commission was read and he addressed the convicts:

What Frobisher, Raleigh, Delaware and Gates did for America, that we are today met to do for Australia, but under happier auspices. Our enterprise was wisely conceived, deliberately devised and efficiently organized; the Sovereign, the Parliament and the people, united to give it their authority, sanction and encouragement. We are here to take possession of this fifth division of the globe on behalf of the British people, and to found a state which, we hope,

became extremely short, supply ships failed to arrive and famine set in. With the arrival of more convict transports — the Second and Third Fleets — there were even more mouths to feed. Then in July 1792 the worst was over. The authorities in London sent assurance that in the future there would be regular shipments of food and other necessities. To all intents and purposes the long years of hunger were now over. Governor Phillip, for reasons of ill health, left the colony on 11 December 1792. When he departed the total population of the colony was 4222: 1256 at Sydney, 1845 at Parramatta and 1121 at Norfolk Island. The number of deaths during his five years in office appears to have been over 1000; 482 of these occurred in 1792, the worst year of the famine.

Governor Lachlan Macquarie

Great changes took place with Governor Phillip's departure. The settlement fell into the clutches of the New South Wales Corps which monopolized trade and prospered at the expense of the people. The 'Rum Corps', as it was soon nicknamed, comprised 21 officers. Extravagant grants of land were made to all officers and they paid for convict labour with rum instead of money, resulting in much drunken debauchery, and illicit stills.

The Governors that followed, despite valiant efforts to smash the corruption and restore law, order and industry, were opposed and their orders not enforced.

On New Year's Day, 1810, Colonel Lachlan Macquarie stepped ashore at Sydney to become the colony's fifth Governor. With him he brought his own regiment, the 73rd, and an order recalling the New South Wales Corps to England. Macquarie's specific task was to 'restore order and tranquillity to New South Wales and to improve the Morals of the colonists, to encourage Marriage, to provide for education, to prohibit the use of Spirituous Liquors and to increase the Agriculture and Stock'.

Meanwhile, other settlements and discoveries had been made. Norfolk Island had been self-supporting since Governor Phillip's time in office.

George Bass and Matthew Flinders had circumnavigated Van Diemen's Land in 1798, and three years later, Flinders, in the *Investigator*, began his journey of charting and circumnavigating Australia. In 1804, convicts, marines and free settlers, under Lieutenant-Colonel David Collins landed at the site of what was to become Hobart, and in the same year Lieutenant-Colonel Paterson formed a settlement that eventually became Launceston. The Van Diemen's Land settlements went through a difficult time; conditions were poor and in 1805 the hardship was intensified by the resettlement of the Norfolk Island people in Van Diemen's Land. But as in New South Wales, relief eventually arrived and the colonists enjoyed a prosperous period. Wool proved profitable, the ship-making industry boomed and whaling and sealing became very lucrative.

Back in Sydney, Macquarie was enforcing his reforms. He opened up a market place, widened streets, organized new storehouses and extensive convict barracks. New methods of Government trading were introduced and free settlers were encouraged to take up farming. In order to abolish the 'rum' trading, Macquarie organized a group of

The old road to Bathurst

settlers to operate a bank which became known as the Bank of New South Wales. Industries grew, whaling and sealing prospered and the wool industry rapidly expanded. The colony's flocks of sheep and cattle were increasing and good pasture was becoming scarce. It was time to move inland.

Several attempts had been made to cross the Blue Mountains. For 20 years after the settlement of Sydney all who sought to cross this barrier reported it as impenetrable.

Then, in 1813, Gregory Blaxland, William Charles Wentworth and William Lawson, accompanied by four horses, four men and five dogs, followed the ridges of the Great Dividing Range and crossed over. The inland climate was found to be perfect for sheep and the development of the Australian wool industry continued apace.

The frontiers of the colony were rapidly pushed back. Men and sheep streamed south-west to the Riverina and Monaro Plains, crossed the Murray and Murrumbidgee, reached south to Port Phillip and north to the Liverpool Plains and the New England district.

But there was still much of Australia to be explored. In 1817 Lieutenant Phillip Parker King surveyed the continent's north coast. A convict and military post was established at Port Essington in 1824 and possession of the north was formally taken. Governor Darling formed settlements on the coast north of Sydney. Towards the end of 1823 John Oxley found the site of Brisbane; a year later this was turned into another penal settlement.

In 1826, the west coast began to open up. Major Lockyer formed a post at Albany, Western Australia, and Captain Fremantle sailed to the Swan River and took possession of all Western Australia in the name of the Crown. Captain James Stirling was appointed Governor and Britain agreed to a business proposition whereby one million acres were to be sold for 1/6d an acre to a business syndicate which was to be responsible for all development and settlement. There were to be no convicts and the migrants were to meet all costs. Most of these investors had never farmed before and settlement proved difficult. In 1849, Western Australia, admitting the need for British finance, became a Crown Colony and transportation of convicts began.

Settlements were springing up around the coast of Australia but one great mystery remained. The

Sturt and his party at Depot Creek, on one of his trips into the interior of the continent

interior. Early explorers were puzzled by the inland rivers they had discovered that flowed to the west. The destination of these rivers became the subject of inland and maritime exploration.

In 1817, John Oxley set out to follow the Lachlan, but returned desolate, concluding that 'the interior of this vast country is a marsh and impenetrable'. In 1828, John Sturt set forth with 11 men, 11 horses, 10 bullocks and a light sailing boat drawn by bullocks on a 4-wheeled carriage. His mission — to find a way around the marshes that had blocked Oxley's progress.

In four and a half months of arduous travelling Sturt solved the riddle of the rivers and dispelled the concept of an inland sea. The Macquarie, Bogan and Castlereagh rivers were defined as tributaries of a great new river flowing south-west — the Darling. Sturt set out again the following year and this time discovered the Murray River. After an eventual journey on this river he and his party saw a 'new and beautiful stream' which he correctly identified as the Darling.

Only one burning question remained. Where did the Murray empty its waters? The expedition left the mouth of the Darling and headed downstream. Fifteen days later Sturt arrived at the termination of the Murray. 'Immediately below me was a beautiful lake which appeared to be a fitting reservoir for that noble stream that had led

The Burke and Wills expedition leaving the Royal Park, Melbourne

us to it, and which was now ruffled by the breeze that swept over it,' he reported. At camp that night they heard the sound of surf breaking behind some low sandhills that separated the lake-side of the sandhills. The party had reached the southern coast, deep in the bight of Encounter Bay. Sturt named the lake after the young princess Alexandrina who was to become Queen Victoria.

The challenge of the interior was being taken up. In 1836 Lieutenant George Grey began an expedition from the vicinity of the Prince Regent River. Here they discovered and named the Glenelg River. On his second expedition he discovered the Gascoyne River and on his return to Perth, found 10 rivers and 2 mountain chains — the Victoria and Gardner's Ranges. One of the

bravest of all Australian explorers, John Eyre, was the first to penetrate central Australia only to be repelled by the 'vast and dreary desert of the interior'. In 1841 he was the first to cross the continent from Adelaide to Albany.

The future for explorers was boundless. John Sturt again took up the gauntlet and in 1844 he led a party north from Adelaide into the interior. Two extensive journeys into the centre took him to Lake Blanche, across the Stony Desert and along the banks of Cooper's Creek. Explorers Edmund Kennedy, Ludwig Leichhardt and Sir Thomas Mitchell were all to explore areas of Australia at this time with varying degrees of success. Mitchell added much to the knowledge of the country that was soon to become Queensland; Kennedy lost his life on the Cape York Peninsula; Leichhardt disappeared with a party of seven men and 77 animals in the interior of Australia.

Perhaps the most tragic of all the early expeditions was that of Robert O'Hara Burke and William Wills who in 1860 set out from Melbourne to cross the country from south to north. Both men were inexperienced explorers and bushmen, but were chosen to lead a government subsidized project that would hopefully put the colony of Victoria ahead of the others in the drive to the interior.

After many mishaps the greatly reduced expedition of eight men reached Cooper's Creek in Queensland. Here they made camp, but the impatient Burke and Wills with two other men left and pushed onwards to the northern coast. They

washed my face and hands in the sea.' He had reached Van Diemen Gulf.

In the 1870s several crossings from east to west had been made and most of the continent had been opened up. It was the end of the age of overland exploration.

Settlement was flourishing. South Australia was founded by an Act of Parliament in 1834. After several years of an unproductive land scheme, it became bankrupt. The British Government intervened and by 1846 wool, grain and some copper mining industries were prospering. Self-government was achieved in 1856.

Adelaide and Perth were idealistic settlements; Sydney, Hobart and Brisbane started out as penal colonies, but Melbourne's origins were commercial. The first permanent settlement was estab-

Cooper's Creek

sighted the tidal waters of the Gulf of Carpentaria, but ill and half starved, with one of the party dying before they returned to the base camp at Cooper's Creek, it was an ill-advised sortie. The rest of the party had abandoned Cooper's Creek, only hours before the return of the three men. Aborigines assisted the weakened and starved men for a time, but death was inevitable. Wills and Burke died and two months later, John King, the only survivor, was found by a rescue party.

John McDouall Stuart was also involved in the race to cross Australia from south to north. After three attempts he finally met with success. In 1861 he set out from Adelaide on a gruelling journey that was to culminate in triumph. On 24 July 1862 a jubilant Stuart wrote: 'I dipped my feet and

lished on the Yarra in 1836 by land seekers John Batman and John Pascoe Fawkner. It developed rapidly as a squatting colony and was incorporated as a town in 1842, two years after the residents first petitioned for the separation of the Port Phillip district from New South Wales.

In these early years the sheep industry was the mainstay of economic growth. Wool was being transported to markets by bullock teams and camel trains. Land was at a premium. By 1845 most grazing land in New South Wales, South Australia, Tasmania and Victoria was occupied. Then the pastoral scene was suddenly shattered. In May 1851 gold was discovered near Bathurst, New South Wales.

Homes were abandoned, labourers walked off

properties, building programmes stopped. Gold fever set in with a vengeance and soon New South Wales and Victoria were dotted with goldfields. The population grew threefold in a decade. The New South Wales goldfields attracted 10 000 eager goldseekers before this tapered off as the rush switched to Ballarat and Bendigo. All ranks of society succumbed to the same thirst for gold. Property in Melbourne went down in value, the streets were empty and deserted and it was impossible to get any work done. Meanwhile the goldfields were ablaze with life.

One gold digger wrote when first seeing the gold town of Ballarat:

> From the margin of the forest a broad swamp spreads, through which the creek runs . . . along this the cradles are ranged for about half a mile, on both sides of the creek and down to the river forming the letter T with the ends upturned. They are crowded so closely together as barely to permit being worked, in some places in triple file.

A tide of immigrants flowed into Victoria — from the neighbouring colonies, and from New Zea-

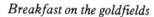

Breakfast on the goldfields

land, England, Europe, the United States, India, China and Ireland. A large criminal element was naturally attracted to the fields and police were few and hard to recruit. Racial tension broke out, the miners objecting to the increasing number of Chinese on the fields. This ultimately resulted in the Immigration Restriction Bill passed by the Commonwealth Parliament in 1901. A fatal clash between the miners and the authorities at Eureka on 3 December 1854 was the culmination of the tension on the goldfields. The affray grew from the diggers increasing resentment of the licensing system and the highhanded attitudes of those who administered it.

Gold was found in all the Australian mainland States and in Tasmania. The largest mass of gold yet found at this time in any land was taken in 1872 from the rocks at Hill End, New South Wales. Known as the Holtermann Nugget, it weighed 234 kilograms with a gold content of 93 kilograms.

The roaring days of gold added excitement and a new dimension to the Australian scene. Shanty towns sprang up and the influx of people of different cultures brought new ideas and contrast to the hitherto rigid colonial society.

When the gold boom petered out, the majority of the diggers turned to the land for sustenance. Crown land was turned into lots. Squatters were allowed to only purchase a small portion of their formerly vast tracts, the remainder being auctioned off. The years following the gold rush were prosperous: mining companies were making large profits; irrigation systems had opened previously infertile areas of land and overseas markets were being found for primary produce.

It was a happy time for everyone until the overseas price for wool fell dramatically in 1886. A long depression began; unemployment was rampant, overseas loans were withdrawn and banks failed. To relieve the pressure the Government brought the banks under its control and changed the legal tender from gold to paper money. After a long difficult period other countries reinvested in Australia and the pressure was eased.

The Government of Australia began to take on a more formal structure. Until 1823, having enormous powers invested in him by the British Government, the Governor of New South Wales was almost omnipotent. In 1823 a nominee council was formed. The Governor, who presided over this council still, however, had the right to veto

Chinamen's huts on the goldfields

any of its decisions. The autocracy of the Governor and the structure of the council underwent various changes over the next few years. Everywhere there was a growing demand for each Colony to have its own revenue and Crown lands. The problem was, who should govern?

In 1850, an Act was passed by the Imperial Government that gave self-government to New South Wales, Victoria, South Australia and Tasmania. In 1859 Queensland became a separate colony from New South Wales and in 1863 South Australia took over control of the Northern Territory which up until then had been administered by New South Wales. Western Australia became a separate colony from New South Wales in 1890.

For many years the need for a Federation was deemed unnecessary. Eventually, however, a constitution was drafted and the Act received royal assent in 1900. Edmund Barton became Australia's first Prime Minister and the first Commonwealth Parliament opened in Melbourne on 9 May 1901.

Australia today is a bustling highly developed nation. Migration has injected new cultures into the more traditional Australian way of life. More than two million people have settled in Australia since 1945 — people from over 30 different countries. Economically Australia still relies on its 170 million sheep. Wool makes up about two-fifths of the country's exports with overall farm products accounting for four-fifths of the total exports.

But, despite the importance of agriculture Australians are one of the most urbanized peoples in the world with six out of every ten people living in one or another of the State capital cities. Australia is a unique land. A land where every Australian can find a life style of his own — whether it is in one of the populous major cities or in the solitude of the outback.

Aboriginal Art

The Aboriginal people of Australia have given us our oldest heritage in the most ancient art forms of the continent. Before the Europeans arrived the Aborigines lived in close harmony with nature. Tribal groupings moved within strictly defined tribal hunting boundaries and the people were exceptionally skilled in hunting and food gathering. They developed a full cultural and ceremonial life and had many philosophical and religious ideas.

Their idea of creation was that in the beginning the world was a lifeless, flat surface from which giant beings eventually arose and journeyed across the plains creating mountains, valleys, rivers and seas. These beings were called the Cult Heroes and they lodged in rocks, trees and waterholes, the unborn spirits of all the animals and Aborigines.

Contact was made with the power of the Cult Heroes through sacred rituals in which painting played a vital role. For instance, the Aborigines retouched the Wandjina paintings in the Kimberleys in West Australia to ensure the continuation of good seasons.

Magic was also an element of Aboriginal art. To increase the food supply, the Aborigine would paint an outline of the animal he wished to hunt. He would then beat the painting with bushes, thus driving out all the spirits who would then take on animal form.

The Aborigines did not attempt to paint a realistic picture of the natural world. The meaning behind the image was significant and painting was, as a result, usually abstract with a concentration of symbols. The artistic implements were

Australia the Sky Hero passed over the earth and took to the sky. In the western desert the Rainbow Serpent or Snake Man carved out the rivers and streams. In the northern Kimberleys the Cult Heroes came from the sea and turned themselves into the rock paintings known as the Wandjina. Two unique art forms are found in the Kimberleys — the Wandjina and the Giro-Giro. The latter, tiny figures of men and women, are believed by the Aborigines to be the work of fairy people. Another fairy people, called the Mimi, are believed to be responsible for the drawings found on the caves and rock-faces of western Arnhem Land. 'X-ray' painting is another highly developed art form in Arnhem Land. Here, on cave faces, the outline, skeleton and internal organs of animals are painted in intricate detail.

Natives kangaroo hunting

provided by nature. Their canvas was a rock face, the bark of a tree, the ground or their bodies. The four basic colours they used were white from gypsum and pipe clay, black earth pigments or charcoal, and yellow and red natural pigments from ochre deposits. Carving tools were a sharpened shell or stone or a possum's tooth. Vegetable fibre and flowers, bird feathers and down and human hair and blood served as decorations.

Although as a whole, Aboriginal art is unique, its forms varied from region to region, as did the names and the forms of the Cult Heroes. In eastern

Bark painting also flourished in this northern area. Purples and browns are added to the four basic colours in this region and most of the bark paintings tell a story or a myth. In central Australia there are no records of bark painting, but here the people excelled in sacred and decorative rock art.

Tree carving was another form of art practised in New South Wales and Queensland. More than 600 carved trees have been recorded and it was believed that these trees were pathways to the earth for the Sky Heroes during sacred ceremonies.

Aboriginal tree carving

The Aboriginal art of rock decorating shows four distinct phases. The earliest forms were simple grooves and lines. In the next phase, outlines of simple subjects such as circles and tortoises were engraved on rock faces. This evolved through to a more formal and symbolic stage until the modern phase was reached when the figures became representative and were chipped out of rock. Much can be learnt about the spirit world of Aboriginal Australia by looking at the visual history, the ancient carvings and paintings that have depicted the world of man and his imagination from far back in time.

Today few Aboriginal artists paint on rock walls; they prefer the medium of bark. In Arnhem Land many Aboriginal families have moved back to their tribal lands, attempting to lead a traditional way of life. The rituals and ceremonies connected with the sacred sites of their ancestors play a significant role in their existence and in this move to maintain a connection with their past, many Aborigines are finding renewed interest in bark painting.

The Land

The most popular image of Australia is that of a sunburnt, parched land with vast empty spaces.

While this is true of a good proportion of the continent it ignores the fact that four out of five Australians live in large coastal cities and towns. To most Australians, the loneliness of the outback has not been experienced.

Climate and distance have determined these settlement patterns. The distances are vast. To fly the 4000-odd kilometres from the east coast to the west coast at the widest point is a greater distance than that between London and Cairo. The size of Australia also means wide climatic contrasts. The lowest temperature ever recorded was $-8°F$ ($-22°C$) at Charlotte Pass, New South Wales, in August 1947; the highest, 127°F (53°C) at Cloncurry, Queensland, in January 1889.

Two-fifths of the continent lie north of the Tropic of Capricorn and severe cyclones occasionally move over the coast bringing violent winds of over 160 kilometres per hour (100 miles per hour) and torrential rain.

Floods and droughts are also common in this continent of extremes. Most of the major rivers are subject to flooding and widespread damage is often caused to farms and towns. Probably the worst flooding in the country's history was in 1852 when the Murrumbidgee River flooded and 89 people drowned. The most severe drought in Australian history lasted from 1859 to 1903 when cattle numbers were reduced by a third and the sheep population cut in half. Drought, after a fairly good season, also brings the terror of bush fires. The worst bush fire catastrophe was in 1939 when 71 people died in one day in Victoria.

Intractable as this land may sound, about 20 per cent of the continent that is occupied by the majority of Australians enjoys a pleasant, temperate climate for most of the year. Sydney, for example, has an average summer temperature of 22.2°C and a winter temperature of 12.2°C.

Rainfall is the key to the climate and land use of the continent. The average rainfall is only about 420 millimetres, compared with a world average of 660 millimetres. Most of this rain falls along the seaward side of the coastal mountain ranges from Darwin to Adelaide and in the south-western area around Perth. The vast areas of desert in the centre and near the head of the Great Australian Bight receive less than 127 millimetres of rain a year.

An aerial cross section of Australia would show a thin green belt of farmland and forest near the sea,

Govett's Leap, in the Blue Mountains

a broken ridge of mountains with grain fields and pastures on their landward slopes, falling into the red barrenness of the Outback extending for about 2500 kilometres until the coastal pattern is repeated again, in reverse.

The mountains of Australia are not especially remarkable for altitude. They reach their highest elevations in the south-east, where the highest peak, Mt Kosciusko, rises 2300 metres above sea level. Also they are all below the perpetual snow-line and have no active volcanoes to enhance their interest. In some far distant ages their height may have been proportionate to their gigantic bulk and in some dim future they may possess a history and romance as thrilling as that which lingers about every crag and peak of Europe and Asia.

The first broad view of the Australian cordillera shows a barrier of over 4000 kilometres in length between two oceans — the Great Dividing Range. These highlands extend from Cape York in the far north to Cape Howe in the south where they turn west and form the Australian Alps.

This long belt of highlands, carved, sculpted and moulded, is made up of rocks of various geological origins and ages. East and west go the waters from its ridge. The fast flowing waters of the former discharge upon the coast and flow into the Pacific Ocean, while most of those that flow to the west wander sluggishly across the great plains of the interior, diminishing in number until they meet the Murray which discharges into Lake Alexandrina and thence to the sea.

The eastern coastal strip, between 50 and 400 kilometres wide, is the most densely populated and agriculturally developed area of Australia. Dairying, mixed farming and meat-raising predominate in the south, while crops of sugar cane, tropical fruits, maize and other cereals are grown in the north.

Vegetation is mainly dense; isolated areas of

rain forest are found and 100 metres high eucalypts tower in dense stands on the Victorian and Tasmanian hillsides.

The seaboard is studded with golden sand beaches, indented river estuaries and large expanses of sheltered water. The largest of the world's coral reefs — the Great Barrier Reef — extends southwards from Torres Strait parallel with the coast for a distance of approximately 2000 kilometres, almost to the 25th parallel. Shoals of brilliantly coloured tropical fish, more than 300 varieties of coral, wooded islands and blue lagoons make the Reef one of Australia's most spectacular attractions.

The Great Dividing Range is the most extensive of Australia's mountain areas but highlands of considerable extent and elevation occur elsewhere. The Flinders Ranges meet the desert in South Australia and, around the continent's south-west fringe, water from the Darling Range feeds onto a narrow coastal plain of limestone and sandstone. The Hamersley Range in the north-west is particularly spectacular, with rock towers and canyons sculpted by sand and wind into fantastic shapes. In the north the Napier Ranges rise in sheer walls, dissected by fast-flowing rivers. Behind them is the highest plateau of Western Australia — the King Leopold Ranges. To the north in this State are the Kimberleys — an area noted for vast cattle stations. The Macdonnell and Musgrave-Warburton Ranges of central Australia are perhaps the most spectacular of all. They support a sparse but unique vegetation and their ground colours are of an unbelievable intensity, ranging from deep blue-black and rich brown hues to brilliant reds, yellows and purples. The towering mesas and jagged ridges of the Australian desert can be compared to no other mountains on earth. Ayers Rock, the world's greatest monolith,

and the rounded massive rocks of the Olgas attract tens of thousands of tourists.

The heartland of Australia is a huge arid and semi-arid plateau; the earth is reddish-brown and vegetation is sparse. The monotony of this area is relieved by the mountainous ridges of rock and by huge salt and mud pans that contain water only after the rare heavy falls of rain. Lake Eyre, the country's largest lake, is one such. The 240-kilometre-long lake, with an area of 8000 square kilometres can fill to a depth of 4 metres after heavy rain, but most of the time it is simply a large area of mud covered with salt. The rivers which drain this immense heartland are also dry for most of the time but after heavy rainfalls they can become raging torrents.

The total output of Australia's rivers is small. One river in India has almost twice Australia's total river flow. The Murray River and its branches comprise the country's largest river system, draining an area almost as big as Texas and California combined. The Murray rises in the Snowy Mountains and flows 2615 kilometres westward before emptying into the Great Australian Bight. The Murrumbidgee and the Darling (Australia's longest river) feed the Murray. The Murray was surrounded with mystery and adventure in the early days of Australia. The Bishop of Ballarat wrote the following lines while strolling alongside the river in the late nineteenth century:

I tread thy brink, Australian Nile,
And in the heated west afar
Glows, where the fierce sun sank erewhile,
Across vast plains, the evening star.
From yonder marsh, the serpent's haunt,
The wild swans rise in dusky cloud;
The bittern's melancholy chaunt
Shrills through the calm air clear and loud.

Wool barge on the Darling River

Another nineteenth century writer opined:

...after seeing the wealth this magnificent stream bears upon its waters and the flocks and herds that are fattened upon its banks, we can hardly repress a sigh of regret that it should not have an outlet worthy of it, so that stately ships might sail in and out and carry their cargoes far into the heart of the country. In such case it might well stand as a rival to the Amazon or Mississippi. Unfortunately, it is without this advantage, its waters struggle to the ocean amid shifting sands and almost stagnant lakes, through channels devious, shallow and difficult, whilst engineering skills seem powerless to provide what nature has failed to give. Whether the defect can be rectified in years to come is yet to be seen. As it is the Murray's course resembles the life of a man of vast strength and talent, who, after a stormy and adventurous youth and a manhood passed in dignity and usefulness, at length in his old age sinks into an obscure grave, unhonoured and imbecile.

Wild Australia

Australia's isolated position and geographical antiquity have led to a vast and unique assortment of flora and fauna. Eucalypts predominate in the Australian bushland. There are more than 500 species. But Australia's national emblem, the wattle has more than 600 indigenous species. The flowers of the wattle range through all shades of gold from pale yellow to deep orange. The wattle derived its name from early English settlers who had previously been used to the practice of 'wattling' — the placing of thin twigs onto a roof to hold a thatch. When they built their homes here they found the acacia branches suitable for this purpose and called the trees 'wattles'.

Grass-trees and baobabs are two of the most unusual trees on the continent. The grass-trees grow in all the Australian States and are called 'blackboys' in Western Australia. The trees have a thick stem forming a short trunk, which often grows to a height of 4 metres. Long rigid leaves resembling coarse grass, grow like a tuft from the crown of this trunk and an elongated flower stem emerges from the tuft. The name 'blackboy' derived from the appearance of the tree after a bush fire. The black, burnt out stump and the elon-

Mallee scrub and kangaroos

gated flower stem resemble an Aborigine carrying a spear.

The baobab is perhaps the most grotesque tree in Australia. Also called the bottle tree, the name is derived from the swelling of the trunk which resembles a giant bottle. This tree has adapted to harsh conditions and has developed an internal storage system for food and water. The base of every branch can yield many litres of drinkable water. The baobab can grow to 12 metres high and its girth has been measured at nearly 18 metres.

Pines, figs, palms, cycads, banksias, mulga scrub, salt bush and wiry spinifex all impart a special character to the regions in which they grow.

Animal life in Australia is rich, varied and unusual. Over 120 different species of marsupial animals are native to the continent. Kangaroos inhabit the open plains where they graze in mobs. The great grey kangaroo is among the largest of the species, sometimes reaching 2 metres in length. Its fur is short and woolly and of a grey brown colour. The great red kangaroo is similar to the grey but has reddish-brown fur with black and white facial markings. The wallaroo is shorter and heavier with brown or black fur. The smaller wallabies prefer the hill and scrub country and are a miniature species. Unique to Queensland are two species of tree kangaroos. These have bluish-

22

grey fur and are about 60 centimetres when fully grown. They spend most of their time on the ground but have hind and fore feet adapted to tree climbing and enjoy leaping and climbing about in the tops of tall trees.

Kangaroos are usually timid creatures but when cornered they will fight fiercely. Kangaroo hunting was a popular sport in the early days of Australia. The following is a late nineteenth-century report of the gruesome pastime:

> The dogs hunt by sight, and the riders keep their eyes open whilst the game is being sought. Once the kangaroo is seen, all the rest is full gallop. The Australian horse may be trusted amongst the broken timber which looks so awkward, and the English visitor had better let the horse have his head, and devote all his attention to sticking on. Very likely the run may be a couple of miles across country. At its close the kangaroo is found 'at bay', and one of the hunters dismounts and hits the animal on the head with a 'waddy', a native name in common use for a short stick. If the animal be an 'old man' he will show fight and prove an ugly customer. An 'old man' will often rip up a dog. The kangaroo dead, it is usual to cut off his tail and ride off with the reeking trophy.

The koala is Australia's second most famous marsupial. This gentle, slow-moving animal has flourished in the eucalyptus forests of Australia for over half a million years. In the first quarter of the century early settlers shot an estimated ten million koalas for their pelts. Today, the koala is strictly protected and special sanctuary areas exist. Gum leaves are the koala's sole food and instead of a tail the furry animal has a calloused pad which enables it to sit comfortably for hours in the fork of a eucalypt tree. The Aborigines named this animal 'koala' meaning 'I don't drink'; the gum leaves supply all the moisture it requires.

The Australian dingo is believed by some archeologists to be the world's oldest dog. The Aborigines domesticated the dingo, calling it the warrigal. The dingo remains in hiding during the day and hunts at night, generally alone or in the company of one other. It has a distinctive bark: a sustained, dismal howl heard only at night. Despite man's many attempts to conquer the dingo this wild dog still has a wide territory in the rough, wooded country of north and central Australia. The dingo was the curse of early settlers and many attempts were made to keep the animal away from the flocks and herds.

Dingoes have never been found in Tasmania, the domain of an outdated marsupial — the Tasmanian devil. An ugly, ferocious creature about 1 metre long, this animal has thick close black fur with white patches, short legs and a short broad muzzle, small eyes and rounded ears. It is untameable, feeding off carrion and preying on other animals.

There are four species of wombat in Australia. These marsupials resemble small bears with short necks, broad heads and short muzzles. The wombat is a nocturnal animal and an active burrower, sheltering in holes during the day and going forth at night to forage for grass, herbage and roots. In common with the majority of Australian marsupials, the wombat has a specialized hind foot. The second and third toes are enclosed in a common skin with little more than the claws separated.

The elusive bandicoot is one of the most interesting marsupials. Resembling a rat with a long tail

The koala, one of Australia's best loved animals

and hind legs like a kangaroo, the bandicoot is a small burrowing animal and is both omnivorous and insectivorous. They are nocturnal; during the day they sleep in nests built in long grass or hollow logs.

The platypus is the paradox of the animal world. Reptile, bird and animal intermingle in the make-up of this freshwater creature but the animal features predominate sufficiently to make it eligible for classification as a mammal. Soft fur, shaded from dark brown to creamy grey, covers the skin which appears many sizes too large for the animal. The head ends in a soft, leathery 'duck bill' structure. Horny ridges take the place of teeth and the paws are webbed, the front ones having webs that extend far beyond the claws.

The creature can only stay underwater for a few minutes and shuts its ears and eyes before submerging. It then uses its extremely sensitive bill to find all its food at the bottom of a pool or river. Its internal organs are also a mass of contradictions. The heart is that of a true animal, but the reproduction organs are virtually identical to those of a reptile. Breeding burrows can reach 18 m in length and at the end of this long tunnel the female platypus lays up to three small, round, soft-shelled eggs. She feeds her young on milk and as she has no teats the babies obtain this milk by sucking it through the pores of her skin.

Although large numbers of platypus were killed in the past they are now totally protected and should survive for many years.

Two-thirds of the 160 species of snakes found in Australia are venomous. The deadliest of all is the taipan found in north Queensland. Rich brown in colour, this snake grows to more than 3 metres and has an elongated square-sided head. The taipan carries enough venom to kill 200 sheep. Its fangs are almost a centimetre long. The small rodents, birds and other small wildlife which constitute its normal diet are killed instantly.

The emu takes precedence of the over-700 species of Australian birds. Unable to fly, the emu can run as fast as a galloping horse. At about 1.5 metres tall it is one of the world's largest birds and is common over much of inland Australia. Found mainly in flocks they live on grass, fruit and insects and build their nests on the ground. When nesting, they shelter in thick scrub and the huge eggs are incubated for two months by the male emu.

Emus, still a familiar sight in many parts of the Outback

The clutch ranges in number up to about nine and when the chicks emerge it is the male who cares for them.

The laughing call of the kookaburra is a familiar sound of the Australian bush. It is a giant kingfisher and preys largely upon rodents and reptiles but has also been known to take small birds. The laughing kookaburra is found in eastern, western and southern Australia and Tasmania. The only other species, the blue-winged kookaburra, which doesn't have a laughing call, is found in the northern part of the continent.

The Australian region is also the headquarters of parrots and cockatoos. There are more than 49 brilliantly coloured species of parrot on the continent and all but one of the world's 12 species of cockatoos are native to Australia.

The Australian waters are the home of more than 2000 different species of fish. Ninety species of shark and 50 species of rays have been recorded in these waters. Perhaps the most unusual of all the freshwater fish is the lungfish of Queensland. A living fossil, this fish can live both on land and in water. As the name suggests, these fish have lungs as well as gills and can obtain oxygen via both sets of organs. The fish has existed essentially unchanged for perhaps 350 million years and specimens as long as 1.5 metres have been taken.

Australia's varied landscape, diverse history and fascinating animals make this a wonderful country for today's Australians to live in and explore and for visitors to experience.

24

Queensland and the Northern Territory

Queensland

CAPTAIN Cook entered Moreton Bay in 1770 and named it after his patron, the Earl of Moreton, then President of the Royal Society. He continued his cruise up the coast until running his ship aground on a coral reef. To make the necessary repairs, Cook beached his vessel and landed where Cooktown now stands. His repairs completed, he sailed as far as Cape York where he hoisted the British colours on Possession Island and proclaimed George III King over all the eastern coast, naming it New South Wales.

The area lay undisturbed until 29 years later when Lieutenant Matthew Flinders in the *Norfolk* dropped anchor in Moreton Bay which he described as 'so full of shoals that he could not attempt to point out any passage that would lead a ship into it without danger'. Two years later he again set out to explore the coast of Queensland, sailing as far as the Gulf of Carpentaria and noting the Great Barrier Reef. Lieutenant King in the *Mermaid* made a further survey of the coast in 1817.

But it was not until 1821 that a serious attempt was made to colonize this area. Botany Bay was becoming overcrowded with convicts and many of the free settlers of the area were beginning to resent contact with convicts and particularly, the emancipists. The British Colonial Office attempted to meet the objections of these settlers by establishing penal settlements in more remote parts of the continent and transferring to them the more intractable felons, especially those who had committed further crimes after being transported to Australia.

Sir Thomas Brisbane, Governor of New South Wales, sent his Surveyor-General, John Oxley, to reconnoitre the virtually unknown country to the north of the Liverpool Plains for suitable sites for penal settlements. He recommended Moreton Bay. In 1824 Brisbane sent a detachment of convicts and troops to Redcliffe. The site, however, was badly chosen and that, combined with the

Captain Cook sighting the Glasshouse Mountains

hostility of the Aborigines, persuaded the party to move to the present site of Brisbane.

At first free settlers were excluded from this newly opened up country but they gradually penetrated the Darling Downs, realizing the rich pastoral potential of the hinterland. Transportation of convicts ceased in 1839 but it was not until 1842 that the district was thrown open to settlement. The great pastoral industry had already been started with the flocks and herds owned by the penal settlement. In 1839 these numbered 900 head of cattle and 4500 sheep. Four years later the cattle had increased to 1620 head and sheep to 12 000. The wool of this flock was sold at 1/– per pound and fetched £1000. The wool industry pushed ahead. In 1840 the first station was established — it was Canning Downs. Two years later the district boasted 43 stations on which grazed 660 horses, 13 295 head of cattle and 184 651 sheep. The population numbered 335, of whom 45 were ticket-of-leave men.

The progress of Queensland was at this stage severely restricted by labour shortages and the northern settlers complained that a fair share of

Emigrants landing in Queensland

Dr John Dunmore Lang

labour in the market did not find its way up to them. In 1849, Dr John Lang, a fiery Presbyterian cleric, inaugurated a scheme for the introduction of free labour, and immigrants were landed for this purpose. But the tension still existed.

The district's centre of Government was Sydney, 965 km south of Brisbane. There were inevitable delays in administration and the officials, of necessity resident in Sydney, did not understand the special problems of the northern settlement. The settlers began to agitate for seperation — the right to run their own affairs. This met with much initial hostility from New South Wales; the *Sydney Herald* of 18 August 1852 said: 'It is difficult to mete out the portions of laughter, pity and contempt which must be awarded to our misguided fellow colonists lying to the northward of the thirtieth degree of latitude'.

The thirtieth degree of latitude was the line of seperation advocated by Lang, spokesman for the separationists. When the British Government granted a constitution to New South Wales in 1842, it had reserved the right to 'erect into a separate colony' any territories north of latitude 26°S, a region about 160 kilometres north of Brisbane. Britain thus envisaged the creation of a northern colony, but had ensured that the Moreton Bay area would be retained by New South Wales.

In 1850 the situation became even more complicated. Another Act was passed whereby the British Government had the power to create a new colony 'northward of 30° of south latitude'. This meant that the proposed colony would include not only Moreton Bay but also the Richmond and Clarence river valleys. The boundary conflicts continued with the separationists insisting that the new colony should include these river valleys.

In 1859 the British Government eventually decided that separation would be desirable and Governor Sir William Denison decided that the boundary between the old and the new colonies should be 29°S as far east as the Barwon and should then follow the natural contours of rivers and mountain ranges to the coast at Point Danger; thus the Richmond and Clarence River areas were to remain part of the colony of New South Wales. The State was called Queensland in honour of Queen Victoria, despite Lang's lobbying for the name of Cookstown. The population was then 23 520.

Queensland was the only one of the six Australian colonies which did not require a separate Act for its establishment. It was created by letters patent on 6 June 1859 and came into actual existence with the arrival of its first Governor, Sir George Ferguson Bowen. Bowen faced the formidable task of having to run a colony with no funds, no police, no civil service and no military force. Fortunately Queensland was so rich in pastoral and agricultural land that it soon established itself on a firm footing. The western plains and tablelands yielded excellent wheat crops and the sugar grown on the rich alluvial flats from the Clarence River in New South Wales to Mossman in the far north soon assumed great economic importance.

Draughting cattle

The first man to grow sugar in Australia was Thomas Alison Scott. In 1823 he interested Governor Brisbane in the possibility of growing cane on a commercial scale and was engaged at £250 a year to establish a plantation at the convict settlement of Port Macquarie. The plantation failed to develop and no further attempt to grow cane was made for several years.

During the 1840s there were a few settlers growing small patches of cane in the Brisbane district. In 1862 another serious attempt to grow cane was mad by Captain Louis Hope. By 1863 he had 20 acres (about 8 hectares) of cane under cultivation at his property at Ormiston, Moreton Bay. His success met with official approval and in 1867 the Queensland Government granted Hope the

then herded into empty holds at gun point. The hatches were battened down against escape. Those who resisted were usually shot. Kidnapping and murder were common. The white population became strenuously divided in its attitude to 'blackbirding', as the recruitment of Kanaka labour was called.

Eventually the Queensland Government was forced to act and in 1868 it passed a Polynesian Labourer Act which decreed recruiting vessels be licensed. The employers of Kanaka labour also had to be licensed and put up a bond against the promise that the men would be returned to their own islands after three years. The importation of labour continued to grow. By 1868 an estimated 22 voyages had been made from Queensland to the

Labour vessel landing Kanakas to work in the sugar fields

right to select 2500 acres (about 1000 hectares) of coastal land for 'his successful demonstrations of the suitability of the Queensland climate to the growth of sugarcane'.

The growth of the sugar industry along with the acute labour shortage that had plagued this northern settlement from its earliest days led to the importing of Kanakas from the surrounding Pacific Islands to do the work.

The methods of recruiting these islanders were open to such abuse that they were to all intents and purposes slaves. Natives were lured aboard schooners by displays of trade goods and were

islands and 2107 Kanakas had been imported. The actual figures were certainly much higher.

By 1881 sugar lands in Queensland totalled nearly 100 000 hectares and it was not until 1904 that indentured labour was banned altogether. According to official estimates, overall 60 000 Kanakas had been recruited from various islands to work the sugar cane. But for them, the sugar industry would never have achieved its present importance in the Australian economy.

The early 1860s saw marked progress in the colony. The Government had negotiated loans from London amounting to £100 850 000, by 1864

Miners panning for gold

telegraph lines had been stretched from the capital to the towns of Maryborough, Gladstone and Rockhampton. In July of the same year the first section of the railway from Ipswich towards the Downs was opened up for traffic. Between 1860 and 1865 about 38 000 immigrants had arrived. A Bank of Queensland with local shareholders and a local directorate was established in 1863. Money was plentiful and credit readily available. Building societies were prospering.

But trouble loomed. The expenditure of borrowed money had been extravagant and this combined with the effect of a depression in Europe, meant money began to run out in the young community of Queensland. Prices of primary products crashed; the Bank of Queensland closed its doors — the treasury was actually empty. Unemployment was rife. The entire organization of the society was tumbling in ruins. Brief respite was gained when Parliament authorized an issue of treasury bills, but it was not until the gold rush that Queensland got back on its feet.

Gold was first found at Canoona on the Fitzroy River in 1858. The richness of the field was greatly exaggerated and almost immediately the field was worked out. Some years passed before fresh discoveries were made, then in quick succession the gold fields of Gympie, Charter Towers, the Palmer, the Etheridge and many others were discovered.

In 1872 a brutally violent chapter of the gold rush history began. The rush to Palmer River from Cooktown began the savage conflict with the Aborigines. The Myall Aborigines waged ceaseless war on the incoming diggers and killed and ate many of them. They particularly sought the

Chinese as they preferred their flesh to that of the European saying 'it was less salty and was equal to the finest bandicoot'. Sporadic warfare also raged between the Chinese and European diggers. The great Mount Morgan field was opened up in 1882. Described as a solid hill of gold, the field's first assay yielded an incredible return of 5700 ounces to the ton, (about 161 500 grams to the tonne). In 1883 there were 15 gold fields being worked forming a total of 7793 square miles (about 18 130 square kilometres).

The next major event in the development of Queensland was the annexation of New Guinea. As early as 1862 an outpost was established at Somerset, on the Queensland side of Torres Strait, and Francis and Alexander Jardine settled there as pearl-fishers and pastoralists. Gold diggers flocked north and began to look even further afield, becoming excited at the prospect of more gold fields in New Guinea. Captain John Moresby claimed eastern New Guinea for Queen Victoria in 1873, but still the British Government was not interested in colonizing the area.

Adventurers continued to drift over to New Guinea in search of gold and at the same time bêche-de-mer fishers began fishing the waters of New Guinea. The Queensland Government decided some control was needed over this new settlement and the Somerset outpost was in 1877 shifted to Thursday Island in Torres Strait. Henry Marjoribanks Chester became resident magistrate and took a lively interest in the future of New

Aborigine throwing a spear

30

Guinea. A roving agent was also appointed by the Queensland Government to patrol the New Guinea waters.

Hostility developed between New Guinea natives and the white men. The 'blackbirders' recruiting human cargoes to work on the sugar plantations aroused much resentment and hostility, as did the bêche-de-mer fishermen. Savage conditions prevailed but still the British Government refused to act.

So, in 1883, the Queensland premier Thomas McIlwraith took matters into his own hands and wrote to Chester ordering him to sail across to New Guinea and take possession of it for Queensland. On 4 April 1883 Chester hoisted the Union Jack at Port Moresby and Australia took possession of its colony. The British Government disowned this annexation for two reason: firstly it suspected that Queensland wanted New Guinea mainly as a source of cheap labour for the cane fields, and secondly it thought that, despite McIlwraith's feelings to the contrary, there was little danger of German intervention in New Guinea.

McIlwraith was defeated at a general election late in 1883 and his successor, Samuel Walter Griffith, was far less forceful in pursuing the annexation of New Guinea. However McIlwraith's predictions proved to be accurate and early in 1884 the German flag was raised on the north-east portion of New Guinea. This time the British Government was prepared to move and in November 1884 the Union Jack was, with the Home Government's blessing, once more hoisted at Port Moresby.

Coco-nut palms at Thursday Island, Torres Strait

The Northern Territory

THE first close examination of the coast of the Northern Territory was made by Matthew Flinders in his circumnavigation of Australia in 1802. He passed through the Darwin area in the *Investigator* at the height of the monsoon season. The average temperature on board was 85°F (29.4°C) and it was higher on shore.

Settlement did not commence in this area until 1823 when station was established at Port Essington for the protection of trader. In 1838 Captain Owen Stanley of the *Britomart* aided the re-establishment of the deserted post and Ludwig Leichhardt in 1844 devoted his energies to its improvement but with no lasting results.

Leichhardt was the first of several intrepid explorers to enter this region. On a visit to Moreton Bay he had heard settlers talk of the land between Jimbour, the most northerly station, and the tiny settlement of Port Essington. When he returned to Sydney Leichhardt determined to explore the region. He selected a party of nine men who would 'patiently submit' to all hardships and would 'resign themselves to my guidance'. As a group the men were absurdly young, had no good knowledge of the bush and were inexperienced with fire arms.

They set out from Jimbour on 1 October 1844 with 17 horses, 16 bullocks, 1200 lb of flour, 200 lb of sugar and 80 lb of tea. Despite becoming lost frequently, the party made steady progress and by Christmas 1844 they had crossed Expedition Range, reached a river which Leichhardt named the MacKenzie and continued north-west through scrubland. It took them six months to reach Burdekin River; they had covered a quarter of the distance to Port Essington.

After struggling over the Great Dividing Range they discovered a river which Leichhardt named the Lynd which ultimately led them to the Mitchell River, the scene of their greatest disaster.

Here, a band of Aborigines savagely attacked their camp, killing one of the party and severely wounding two others.

However the party pressed on and reached the sea on 5 July 1845. They proceeded along the coast of the Gulf of Carpentaria and began traversing the base of Arnhem Land. They were short of food, in pitiful health and exhausted. After crossing Alligator River they finally came across a cart track which took them in to Port Essington on 17 December 1845. They had travelled for 14 months and 17 days and traversed 4800 km.

About the same time as Leichhardt was making his journey, another explorer, Charles Sturt, penetrated the south-eastern desert of the Northern Territory. He had forwarded a plan to the Colonial Office, which he claimed would enable the whole of the interior of Australia to be explored within two years. His expedition left Adelaide on 10 August 1844, and consisted of 15 men, a boat and carriage, 5 carts, 11 horses, 30 bullocks and 20 sheep. After a journey of much hardship — the heat was so intense that a thermometer graded to 127°F (about 53°C) burst — they reached as far north as Birdsville and turned back. Sturt's journey took one year and five months. 'I reached my home at midnight on the 19th of January,' Sturt wrote, 'and on crossing the threshold, raised my wife from the floor on which she had fallen.'

Augustus Gregory was another explorer with a brave plan. He decided to sail to the mouth of the Victoria and then travel eastward overland. He reached Point Pearce at the mouth of the Victoria in September 1855. Gregory began to work his way cautiously upstream in his vessel the *Tom Thumb*, but the schooner eventually ran aground on a sand bank and was badly damaged. So, on the 3 January 1856 Gregory set off overland with 7 men and 30 horses to follow the river south.

The countryside did not appear very promising: 'The horizon was unbroken,' wrote Gregory, 'all

Stuart's tree, on which he cut his initials to record the feat of crossing the continent from south to north

appeared one slight undulating plain with just sufficient triodia spinifex and bushes growing on it to hide the red sand when viewed at a distance.' They returned to the depot camp and arranged for the *Tom Thumb* to sail to a rendezvous at the mouth of the Albert River in the south-east corner of the Gulf of Carpentaria. The land party then sett off, reached the Alber River and as there was no sign of the *Tom Thumb* they headed onwards, eventually reaching the coast at Port Curtis.

The botanist von Mueller, who travelled with the party, gave a good account of an explorer's typical day.

> We were roused precisely at 4 a.m. by the last sentry on watch. Finished our simple breakfast in a quarter of an hour, went at once in search of our horses, and managed generally to have them caught, driven in, saddled and packed a little past sunrise. We travelled hardly ever less than eight hours, often ten at the rate of 3 m.p.h., but when grass and water was not conveniently found, sometimes considerably longer. Unloading, going through our little domestic duties, repair of clothes, pitching our calico tents and refreshing ourselves with a hasty meal would occupy us for better than an hour... At night we stretched ourselves on our blankets and generally in full clothes, to be ready for defence at a second's notice, the gun alongside, the revolver under our head.

Parts of the Northern Territory had been explored but it was not until John McDouall Stuart made his epic journey northward from Adelaide in 1862 that anything was definitely known about the interior.

Stuart was the first man to reach the geographical centre of Australia and to carry on from there to reach the North Sea. He had been part of Sturt's 1844 expedition into the interior and had learnt a great deal about survival techniques. South Australia was anxious to be the first to launch an expedition to cross Australia and find 'the most practicable route for the overland cable intended to unite this continent with India and Europe'. Parliament agreed to pay £2000 to 'the first person who will succeed in crossing from the colony to the shores of either the north-west or northern portion of the Australian continent'.

Stuart left Chambers creek on 2 March 1860. He had with him 2 men and 13 horses. He pressed steadily onwards, and named the Finke, 'a huge gum creek', and also Chambers Pillar. They crossed and named the Hugh River and had their first glimpse of the Macdonnell Ranges. On 22 April Stuart wrote, 'I am now camped in the centre of Australia.' All were sick and suffering from scurvy but they were determined to proceed and by early June had discovered Tennant Creek. After a skirmish with about 100 Aborigines Stuart returned to Adelaide.

During the next few weeks Stuart assembled a party of 10 men and with financial assistance from the Government headed north again in early January 1861. He travelled further north than his first expedition but was halted by dense scrub areas; 'a complete stop to further progress; from there I feel it is hopeless case either to reach the Victoria or the Gulf. The plains and forest are as great a barrier as if there had been and inland sea or a wall built round.'

Despite many attempts to penetrate further, Stuart was forced to head back to Adelaide.

On 8 January 1862, a month after his return, prompted by the South Australian Government and with more financial assistance Stuart was off again with an expedition of 10 men and 71 horses. On 11 March he reached the centre of Australia and a month later Newcastle Waters, the most northerly point of his last expedition. After five weeks of desperately trying to find a way through to the Victoria or Adelaide Rivers Stuart wrote; 'To make the Victoria through the country I have just passed into would be impossible. I must now endeavour to make the Roper.'

After moving slowly north from waterhole the party came across a stream heading norhtwards and they began to move steadily forwards. On 25 June they reached the Roper River. Stuart had been instructed to reach the Victoria or Adelaide Rivers so instead of following the Roper to the sea they headed north over fast-flowing streams (Stuart named one of them the Katherine) and rocky ranges. Further north he found what he

repeat the call before they fully understood what was meant. Hearing which they immediately gave three long and hearty cheers. The beach is covered with a soft blue mud, it being ebb tide, I could see some distance . . ., I dipped my feet and washed my face and hands in the sea as I promised the late Governor Sir Richard MacDonnell I would do if I reached it.

Stuart cut his intials into a large tree and hoisted the Union Jack.

An Aboriginal encampment

thought was the Adelaide but he was mistaken.

After pushing their way north on 24 July Stuart noted in his diary:

> Crossed the valley and entered the scrub which was a complete network of vines. Stopped the horses to clear a way while I advanced a few yards on the beach and was gratified and delighted to behold the waters of the Indian Ocean in Van Diemen's Gulf, before the party with the horses knew anything of its proximity. Thring who rode in advance of me called out 'The sea;' which so took them all by surprise and were astonished that he had to

His successful exploration gave fresh impetus to settlement. In 1864 Finniss made an attempt at establishing a colony at Escape Cliffs near the mouth of the Adelaide River. Ineffective rule, troublesome natives and an ill-chosen site soon resulted in disorganization. It was not until 1869 that the town of Palmerston (later to become Darwin) was laid out on the shores of Port Darwin and a well-defined beginning made to colonization. Pastoralists in search of new land followed in the explorer's foot steps and mineral discoveries were made which encouraged speculative efforts at permanent settlement. The country was harsh and only the toughest settlers survived.

Officially the Northern Territory was still part of New South Wales but the Government of New South Wales did not have the desire nor means to administrate it. Queensland, on the advice of the explorer Gregory, obtained permission to extend its boundaries in 1862, taking in the fertile Barkly Tableland. The Government also indicated to London that it would be prepared to annex the rest of the Northern Territory, with the proviso that they would not be prepared to undertake finanicial reponsibility for the whole area. Their request was denied. John McDouall Stuart's report to the South Australian Parliament made them realize that the acquisition of this region could be profitable as there many large tracts of potentially good cattle country. The South Australian Government accordingly applied to London to annex the Northern Territory and in May 1863 their request was granted.

The overland telegraph between Adelaide and Port Darwin was completed in 1872 and the line not only opened up the Northern Territory but also gave explorers a point of reference. In 1873, a Government Surveyor, William Christie Gosse, set out from the telegraph station at Alice Springs, passed through some flat spinifex country and was amazed to see a huge rock monolith rising out of the plain. He wrote: This seems to be a favourite resort of the natives, judging from the numerous camps in every cave. They amuse themselves covering these with all sorts of devices — some of snakes very cleverly done, other of two hearts joined together; and in one I noticed a drawing of a creek with an emu track going down the centre.

He called his discovery Ayers Rock after the Governor of South Australia, Sir Henry Ayers.

In 1873 the settlement of Port Darwin swelled with the influx of Chinese labour to the gold fields. When the Palmer gold field in north Queensland began to decline Chinese merchants in Australia recruited Chinese labour and Hong Kong skippers began to land their passengers at Darwin, the nearest port for the newly opened field at Pine Creek. Conditions were extremely sever in the Northern Territory and mine directors asserted that the only hope for the industry lay in the employment of coolie labour.

Chinese and Malayans were brought to Darwin, fed on rice and fish and paid 8 Straits dollars a month — one-twelfth of the wages paid to

An inland telegraph station

European miners. By 1879 Chinese in the Northern Territory outnumbered Europeans by seven to one.

Life in the small settlement of Darwin was fairly quiet during these years, although the cable did much to ensure the community's stablility. A nineteenth-century colonist wrote:

Port Darwin being the terminus of the British Australia cable, the officials required to work it are a large factor in the population and are noted for their social qualities and unbounded hospitality to visitors. Through their little office passes all the news that makes the rest of Australia quiver with exultation or despondency and the negotiation of a loan or success of a Beach reaches the continent at this far-away speck on its surface. Another office transmits the messages thus received to Adelaide by the trans-continental telegraph the construction of which involved an immense outlay of time, pluck and expenditure. A resident magistrate controls the affairs of the infant country to some extent but as every step must be sanctioned by the Government he is not such an autocrat as one could imagine. Three or four public houses (all built on piles to stay the ravages of white ants, which are one of the serious hindrances to the settlement of the country) and the same number of stores and banks are the principal buildings in the township which is laid out and surrounded by reserves.

By the late 1890s railways had been built from Darwin to Pine Creek and from Adelaide to Oodnadatta. However, the isolation and extreme climate of the Northern Territory severely hampered the success of developmental enterprises and gravely embarrassed South Australia and in 1911 the Commonwealth Government took over.

Places of interest

QUEENSLAND

Brisbane and environs

Anzac Memorial and Eternal Flame
Art Gallery,
   160 Ann Street,
   Brisbane

Botanic Gardens, Mount Coot-tha
Botanic Gardens,
   Alice Street,
   Brisbane
Bunya Park

City Hall,
   King George Square,
   Brisbane

Earlystreet Historical Village, Norman Park

Festival Hall,
   65 Charlotte Street,
   Brisbane

Griffith University,
   Kessels Road,
   Nathan

Lone Pine Sanctuary

Moreton Bay Islands
Moreton Island
Mount Coot-tha

Newstead House — historic house,
   Breakfast Creek

Oasis Gardens
Observatory,
   Wickham Terrace,
   Brisbane
Old Government House (Queensland Institute
   of Technology),
   George Street,
   Brisbane

Parliament House,
   Alice Street,
   Brisbane

Parliament House Annexe

Queen Elizabeth II Jubilee Sports Centre,
   Nathan
Queensland Art Gallery,
   160 Ann Street,
   Brisbane
Queensland Museum,
   Gregory Terrace,
   Brisbane

State Library,
   William Street,
   Brisbane
St John's Cathedral,
   Ann Street,
   Brisbane
St Stephen's Cathedral,
   Elizabeth Street,
   Brisbane
Stradbroke Island

University of Queensland,
   St Lucia

Beyond Brisbane

Atherton Tableland
Australian Sugar Museum, Mourilyan

Barakula State Forest
Barrier Reef
Barron Falls
Bellenden Ker National Park
Birdsville Track
Blackdown Tableland Forestry Reserve
Bookera Lagoon Wildlife Sanctuary
Bribie Island
Buderim Ginger Factory,
   Buderim
Bunya Mountains National Park
Burleigh Heads Fauna Reserve

Callide Fish Hatchery
Callide Power Station
Cape York Peninsula
Captain Cook Memorial, Point Danger

Carnarvon National Park
Channel Country
Chillagoe Caves National Park
Cooloola National Park
Conway Range National Park
Cotton Ginnery, Blioela
Cunningham's Gap National Park
Currumbin Bird Sanctuary

Darling Downs
Dunk Island

Eungella National Park

Fassifern Valley National Park
Fraser Island

Girraween National Park
Gladstone — mining, industrial and shipping centre
Glasshouse Mountains
'Gold Coast'
Great Barrier Reef
Gulf Country

Helidon Spa
Heron Island National Park
Hinchinbrook Island National Park

James Cook University, Townsville
Jondaryan Woolshed — historical museum,
    near Toowoomba

Lake Barrine National Park
Lake Eacham National Park
Lamington National Park
Lindeman Island National Park
Lizard Island National Park

McPherson Ranges
Mount Bartle Frere
Mount Glorious National Park
Mungana Caves
Mystery Craters, near Gin Gin

Noosa National Park
Nerada Tea Plantation

Offshore Islands

Palmerston National Park
Pioneer Village, Laidley

'Snowy Mounts' salt fields, near Rockhampton

Tamborine Mountain National Park
Teewah Coloured Sands Cliffs
Thursday Island
Tinaroo Falls

Wallaman National Park
Whitsunday Passage Islands
Winery, Romaville

Wivenhoe Dam
Yowal Opal Fields, near Eulo

NORTHERN TERRITORY

Darwin and environs

Botanic Gardens,
    Gardens Road,
    Darwin

Catholic Cathedral,
    90 Smith Street,
    Darwin
Civic Centre,
    Harry Chan Avenue,
    Darwin
Chinese Temple,
    Woods Street,
    Darwin
Christchurch Cathedral,
    2 Smith Street,
    Darwin

East Point War Museum,
    East Point

Government House,
    Government House Esplanade,
    Darwin

Leichhardt Memorial,
    The Esplanade,
    Darwin

Museum and Art Gallery,
    Mitchell Street,
    Darwin
Music Bowl,
    Botanic Gardens,
    Darwin

Olympic Pool,
    Ross Smith Avenue,
    Fannie Bay

Public Library,
    The Esplanade,
    Darwin

Ross Smith Memorial,
    Ross Smith Avenue,
    Fannie Bay

Beyond Darwin

Arltunga Historical Reserve, near Alice Springs
Arnhem Land Aboriginal Reserve
Ayers Rock
Ayers Rock-Mount Olga National Park

Berry Springs

'Devil's Marbles', near Wauchope
'Devil's Pebbles', near Tennant Creek

Ewaninga Rock Carvings

Finke River Gorge National Park
Flying Doctor Service Base,
    Alice Springs
Fogg Dam Reserve

Glen Helen Gorge
Gove Peninsula

Henbury Meteorite Craters
Hermannsburg Mission
Howard Springs

John Flynn Memorial Church,
    Todd Street,
    Alice Springs

Kakadu National Park
Katherine Gorge
Katherine Gorge National Park

Kings Canyon

Marrakai Plains
Mataranka Pool Reserve

Nobles Nob open cut gold mine
Nourlangie Rock

Okiri Rock
Olgas, The
'Organ Pipes', Finke River
Ormiston Gorge
Ormiston National Park

Palm Valley
Pitchi Richi native bird and flower sanctuary and
    pioneer museum

Rum Jungle

School of the Air,
    Head Street,
    Alice Springs
Simpson's Gap National Park
Springvale Homestead — historic house,
    near Katherine
Standley Chasm

Telegraph Historical Reserve, Alice Springs
The Olgas

Uluru National Park

West McDonnell Ranges National Park

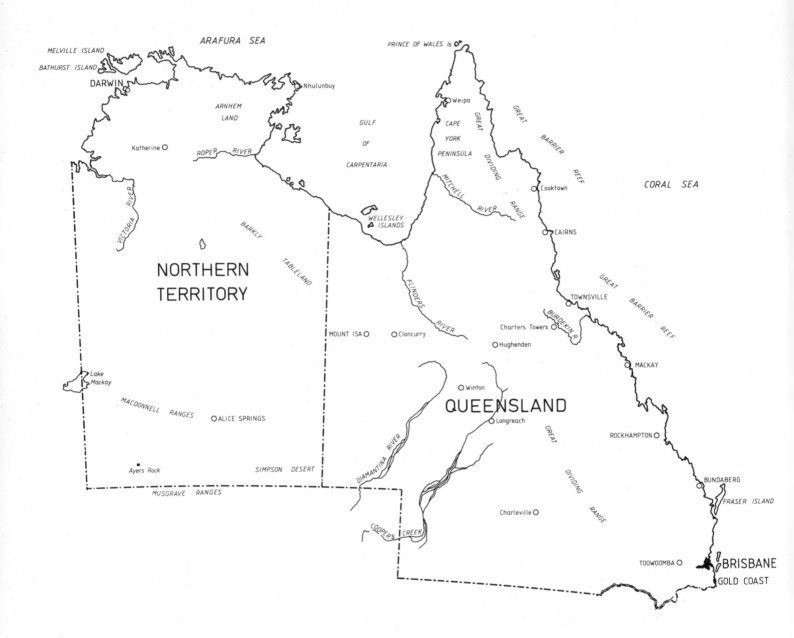

ARAFURA SEA

MELVILLE ISLAND
BATHURST ISLAND

DARWIN

PRINCE OF WALES Is.

Nhulunbuy

Weipa

ARNHEM
LAND

CAPE
YORK
PENINSULA

Katherine

ROPER   RIVER

GULF

OF

CARPENTARIA

GREAT

GREAT

BARRIER

REEF

CORAL SEA

Cooktown

VICTORIA   RIVER

BARKLY

TABLELAND

WELLESLEY
ISLANDS

MITCHELL

RIVER

DIVIDING

RANGE

CAIRNS

NORTHERN
TERRITORY

FLINDERS

RIVER

TOWNSVILLE

GREAT

BARRIER

REEF

Charters Towers

BURDEKIN R.

MOUNT ISA

Cloncurry

Hughenden

MACKAY

Lake
Mackay

Winton

QUEENSLAND

MACDONNELL   RANGES

ALICE SPRINGS

Longreach

ROCKHAMPTON

GREAT

Ayers Rock

SIMPSON   DESERT

DIAMANTINA RIVER

DIVIDING

RANGE

BUNDABERG

FRASER ISLAND

MUSGRAVE   RANGES

Charleville

COOPERS   CREEK

TOOWOOMBA

BRISBANE

GOLD COAST

The city of Brisbane, Australia's third largest city. (Higgins)

Storey Bridge, from the old Botanic Gardens, Brisbane. (Higgins)

The Queensland Cultural
Centre overlooks the
Brisbane River. (Higgins)

Glistening sands at
Currumbin on the Gold
Coast. (Solness)

The Gold Coast is a mecca
for those who enjoy water
sports of all varieties.
(Higgins)

▽ Rainbow Bay,
Coolangatta. (Wigney)

Parasailing at Southport
on the Gold Coast.
(Higgins)

Fishermans Wharf, Main
Beach, on the Gold Coast.
The Gold Coast caters for
around 3 million visitors
each year. (Higgins)

Parrots at the Currumbin
Bird Sanctuary on the Gold
Coast. Founded in 1947,
the Sanctuary is now part of
the National Trust.
(Queensland Tourist &
Travel Corporation)

Surf lifesaving boats take
to the turbulent waters on
a Gold Coast beach.
(Queensland Tourist
& Travel Corporation)

The Big Pineapple at
the Sunshine Plantation,
115 kilometres from
Brisbane. The 16 metre
high replica of a pineapple
contains a Polynesian-style
restaurant, tropical market
and observation deck.
(Queensland Tourist
& Travel Corporation)

The Big Cow at the Sun
Coast Dairy on the Bruce
Highway. Visitors may
enter the Big Cow to view
audio visual displays on the
dairy industry. (Queens-
land Tourist & Travel
Corporation)

Coolum Beach on the
Sunshine Coast.
(Queensland Tourist &
Travel Corporation)

Six hundred metres above sea level, a cave at Lamington National Park frames cool rainforest, ferns and orchids. Large stands of Antarctic beech found growing here are thought to be evidence that a great southern continent, which included Australia, Antarctica, Africa, South America and India, once existed. (Dawes)

Undulating peaks of the Great Dividing Range stretch into the horizon near the Queensland – New South Wales border. (Dawes)

Heron Island, a true coral cay, is a nesting place for terns, gulls, muttonbirds and turtles. Over 1000 varieties of fish and 200 varieties of coral inhabit its reefs. (Higgins)

△
◁ *Fraser Island, the largest*
◁ *island off Queensland's*
coast and the largest sand
island in the world, is a
unique area of freshwater
lakes, tangled rainforest,
swamp and heath vege-
tation and endless beaches.
(Solness, Green)

A memorial to Captain
Cook, the billowing sails,
mast and rigging of the
Singing Ship at Emu
Park. The free-form spire
has concealed organ pipes
which echo the varying
moods of the wind.
(Higgins)

Sparkling seascape at ▷
Yeppoon, main commercial
centre of the Capricorn
Coast, Queensland.
(Higgins)

A quiet corner of solitude at Gladstone Harbour, Queensland's largest tonnage port. (Higgins)

Picking pineapples at a plantation on the Sunshine Coast. (Queensland Tourist & Travel Corporation)

The First Fleet brought sugar cane to Australia from South Africa in 1788. Large scale cultivation began near Brisbane in 1864 and the industry spread rapidly up the coast. (Solness)

Salt flats near Bajool.
The Fitzroy River delta
between Bajool and Port
Alma holds subterranean
brine which is pumped to
the surface into ponds.
Once a year, after solar
evaporation, the salt is
harvested and stacked in
tall white stock piles known
as the 'Snowy Mounts'.
(Solness)

One of the natural wonders
of the world — the Great
Barrier Reef. More than
300 varieties of coral and
brilliantly coloured tropical
fish endow this 2000 kilo-
metre-long reef with more
life to the square centimetre
than anywhere else on
earth. (Higgins)

Cook's Pillar, Cooktown.
Captain Cook beached here
in 1770 to repair damage
after running aground on
the Barrier Reef. (Solness)

South Molle Island, in
the heart of the beautiful ◁
Whitsunday Passage. ▷
(Solness)

Castle Hill stands sentinel over Townsville, the major city of north Queensland. (Solness)

Coral islands, north Queensland. (Higgins)

They're riding them hard at Proserpine rodeo, Queensland. (Solness)

Overleaf: Lush vegetation on Hinchinbrook Island just south of Tully, where more than 500 centimetres of rain fall each year — Australia's highest rainfall. (Solness)

Lake Eacham, a crater lake 730 metres above sea level in the Atherton Tableland. (Solness)

Sooty terns cover the sky at the breeding sanctuary of Michaelmas Cay off the coast near Cairns. (Solness)

Grandeur at Barron Gorge, Atherton Tableland. (Solness)

Millstream Falls — at 65 metres wide, they are the widest falls in Australia. (Solness)

Cairns, one of Australia's major sugar-shipping ports and the centre for north Queensland tourist traffic. (Solness)

The Daintree River flows through verdant country in north Queensland. (Green)

A bird's eye of view of Cairns airport is obtained from the northern hills of the Botanic Gardens. (Solness)

Millaa Millaa Falls, west of Innisfail. (Solness)

The rarely used Northern Territory – Queensland border crossing on the Gulf Road. (Green)

Smoke from surrounding bush fires almost engulfs a road train as it relentlessly plies its way through remote Gulf country. (Solness)

Petrol or hamburger? A passing emu stops for refreshment at the Camooweal Roadhouse. (Solness)

The thinly populated town of Normanton in the Gulf country. In the gold days of 1891 the town had a population of 3000; now there are 800. (Solness)

Charred and smoking remains of a bush fire in the Gulf country. (Solness)

The Normanton to Croydon railway must be one of the most unique in the world. The train is a converted London bus that was brought to the area in the 1930s and is still operating. (Green)

The Normanton Railway
Station. (Green)

Cooper's Creek, Queens-
land. The site of the last
camp made by Robert
O'Hara Burke and
William John Wills on their
tragic overland journey
from Melbourne to the Gulf
of Carpentaria in 1860/61.
(Green)

A twentieth century carving
of Robert Burke on a tree at
Cooper's Creek. (Green)

Water seepage flooded this old mine near Mary Kathleen in the Mt Isa district. (Solness)

Cockatoos congregate in a tree at Boulia. This bird is widespread in the timbered regions of northern and eastern Australia. (Dawes)

Termite mounds dot the landscape between Normanton and Burketown. (Solness)

A rich silver-lead deposit was discovered at Mt Isa by John Campbell Miles in 1923. He named the area after his sister, Isabella. Today Mt Isa Mines operate one of the largest silver-lead mines in the world. Copper and zinc are also mined and processed here. (Solness)

Fannie Bay, Darwin, is the site where Keith and Ross Smith landed their aircraft in 1919, completing the first flight from the UK to Australia. (Higgins)

The residence of the Northern Territory Administrator, Darwin. Built in 1870, this is one of the few buildings that has withstood the ravages of World War II bombing and Cyclone Tracy. The Northern Territory obtained self-government in 1978 and became, in effect, Australia's seventh State. (Higgins)

The Old Victoria Pub in Smith Street — Darwin's favourite watering hole. (Higgins)

Festival time in Darwin. (Higgins)

Overleaf: Sweeping coast-line leading to Darwin Harbour — the only port on the north coast. (Higgins)

East Alligator River Crossing, the entrance to the 8 million hectare Arnhem Land Aboriginal Reserve, is a popular fishing spot. (Higgins, Dawes, Andrews)

The dingo, Australia's only species of wild dog, was probably brought into the country by the Aborigines. (Dawes)

The pelican is found throughout Australia wherever suitable areas of water exist. (Higgins)

Jabiru, Arnhem Land. (Dawes)

Fire rages through bush near Mataranka. (Dawes)

Nourlangie Rock in the Kakadu National Park is an art gallery of Aboriginal rock paintings. (Dawes, Higgins)

Extraordinary mounds, as high as small trees, dot the landscape in the 'Top End' of the Northern Territory. The rock-hard mounds of digested mud are constructed by termites. (Higgins)

Steam forms a cloud over the beautiful hot springs at Douglas, south of Darwin. (Higgins)

Aboriginal children, Arnhem Land. (Higgins)

*Edith Falls at Edith River,
east of Katherine.
(Higgins)*

*Pandanus line the banks
along a peaceful stretch of
the Katherine River.
(Higgins)*

◁ ▷

One of the major attractions of the Northern Territory is the Katherine Gorge National Park where the river flows between towering, brilliantly coloured walls. Aboriginal rock paintings form huge murals high above the flood level on the gorge walls. (Higgins)

The Devils Marbles —
a cluster of gigantic
boulders piled up on each
other. Aboriginal legend is
that the boulders are eggs
laid by the mythical Rainbow Snake. (Solness)

Simpsons Gap National
Park, west of Alice
Springs. (Solness)

Magnificent scenery at
Ross River. Ancient fossils
and Aboriginal carvings
believed to be more than
30 000 years old can be
found in this area.
(Higgins)

Sculptures by William Ricketts at 'Pitchi Richi' museum, Alice Springs, depict the Dreamtime of the Aboriginal people. (Higgins)

The thick-walled stone buildings of the old Telegraph Station at Alice Springs. Site of the original township, settlement began here when the station was built to transmit messages across the continent, via the Overland Telegraph. (Solness)

Palm Valley in the Finke Gorge National Park — tropical refuge for cycad palms and the 5000-year-old Livistona mariae palms. (Higgins)

Dry and barren countryside east of Alice Springs. An average rainfall of only 24 millimetres falls in the central area of the Northern Territory. (Solness)

The heat and dust of rodeo time at Alice Springs. (Dawes)

The 'Jewel of the Centre' — Ormiston Gorge reflected in the still waters of the Finke River. (Dawes)

Ghost gums cling preci- ▷
pitously to the cliffs of ◁
Ormiston Gorge. (Higgins)

*Blackboys and dusty red
dirt roads at Gosse Bluff on
the eastern border of the
Lake Mackay Aboriginal
Land. (Higgins, Dawes)*

Glen Helen Gorge on the Finke River in the West Macdonnells. (Higgins)

The Organ Pipes rising above the Finke River, one of the oldest watercourses in the world. (Higgins)

Fact and fantasy in the Macdonnell Ranges: top, a group of wild donkeys; middle, the strange formation of Lizard Rock; and, bottom, a charred stump gazes across the slopes. (Dawes)

Katatjuta — the Olgas — literally 'place of many heads', is a spectacular group of massive rock domes rising steeply from the level desert in the 'Red Centre' of Australia. The 30 domes are separated by narrow vertical chasms and the highest point is 450 metres above the spinifex plain. (Higgins, Dawes)

Chambers Pillar, Central ▷ Australia, was first sighted by John McDouall Stuart in 1860 and named by him for James Chambers who financed the expedition. Many explorers of the period have carved their name on the sandstone monolith. (Higgins)

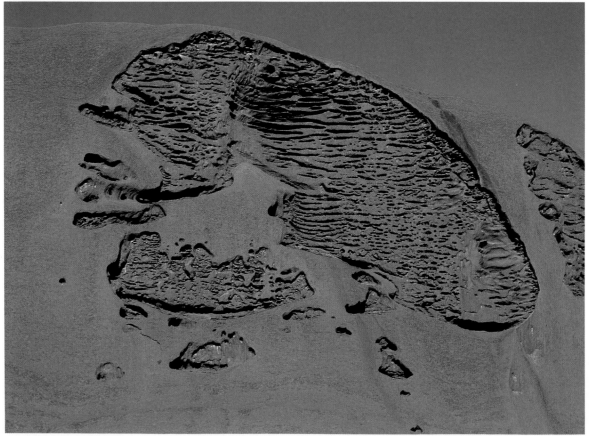

Ayers Rock, the world's largest monolith, rises 348 metres above the plain and is 9 kilometres in circumference. The sheer immensity of this great rock and the unusual colouring, which changes from orange to purple at sunrise and sunset, has made it one of the natural wonders of the world. A sacred dreaming place of the Aboriginal people, the base of the rock is undercut with caves in which the Aboriginals have left galleries of rock paintings in charcoal and ochre. (Dawes, Higgins)

The Brain — an unusual formation on the face of Ayers Rock. (Higgins)

A rope walk assists the adventurous on the 348 metre climb to the summit of Ayers Rock. (Solness)

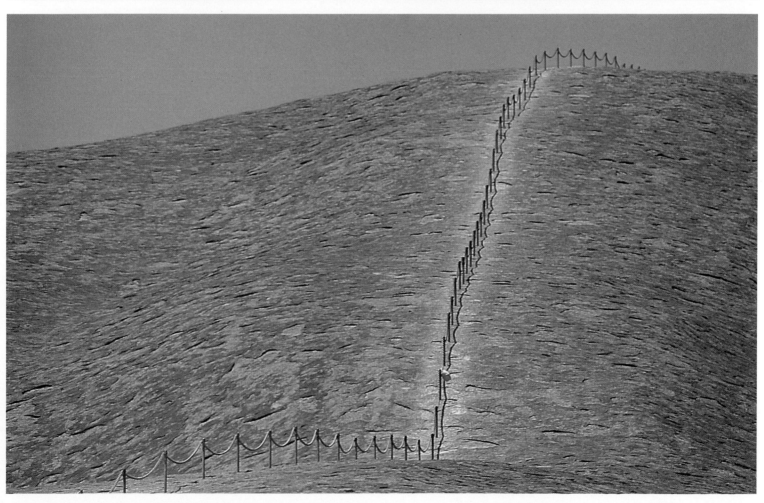

103

*Spectacular beauty
at Kings Canyon which
stretches for almost 2 kilometres with pastel-coloured
sandstone walls on either
side, reaching a height of
over 200 metres. (Solness,
Dawes)*

New South Wales

New South Wales

IN 1768 James Cook in HMS *Endeavour* set sail from England with a party of scientists to observe the transit of Venus from a favourable vantage point in Tahiti. His assignment complete, he sailed south, circumnavigated the north and south islands of New Zealand and then headed west in search of the unknown New Holland. Nineteen days sailing brought him to the coast of Australia at a place Cook named Point Hicks. 'It had,' he said, 'a very pleasing appearance' and as he sailed northwards his delight in this unknown continent increased. He landed at

had been aroused by Cook's discoveries but it was not until Britain lost her American Territories in the War of Independence that there was any urgency to colonize the area. In England in the middle of the eighteenth century a large number of crimes — such as pick pocketing — carried the death sentence. However, a surprising degree of leniency was shown by magistrates and these sentences were often commuted to transportation.

America had been the dumping ground for these transported convicts, but after the war America was no longer available and the British

The Heads, Sydney Harbour

Botany Bay on 29 April 1770. Here Cook first came across the Aborigines who fled at the first approach of the white men. Cook sailed further north and after turning westward through Torres Strait he formally proclaimed British sovereignty over the whole east coast of the continent 'from latitude 38°S to this place 10½°S'. He called it New South Wales.

By 1779 practically the whole coast of Australia had been at least cursorily explored. Much interest

jails became hopelessly crowded. The British Government had to take action and on 18 August 1786 Lord Sydney signed a letter to the Lord Commissioners of Treasury that stated that 'His Majesty . . . has been pleased to signify to me his royal commands that measures should immediately be pursued for sending out of this kingdom such convicts as are under sentence or order of transportation.'

Action was speedily taken and the first 750 con-

The first landing place, Botany Bay

victs were embarked in transports during the first five months of 1787. Captain Arthur Phillip was appointed to organize the project and become the colony's first governor. The First Fleet was made up of the 520-ton HMS *Sirius*, her consort the *Supply*, six ships transporting the convicts — the *Alexander, Charlotte, Lady Penrhyn, Prince of Wales, Friendship* and *Scarborough*, and the supply ships, the *Borrowdale, Fishburn* and *Golden Grove*. The voyage of 24 000 kilometres took 8 months.

Captain Phillip first examined Botany Bay, but found it inadequate. He moved north to Port Jackson, 'and had all the satisfaction of finding the finest harbour in the world, in which a thousand sail of the line may ride in perfect security'. About 6 kilometres up the harbour on the south shore he found a cove with excellent anchorage and chose this as the site of his first settlement. He named it Sydney, after the Home Secretary, Lord Sydney.

On 26 January 1788 Phillip raised the Union Jack over the encampment, toasts were drunk and musket volleys fired. The task of founding a settlement had began. Times were difficult: few convicts were used to manual labour; there was a great deal of drunkenness and immorality; and there was little fertile land near the settlement and crops dried up in the heat.

Early in March, Phillip set out to explore the hinterland in the hope of finding more fertile land, but except for a few isolated pockets he found little arable land. Winter increased the difficulties, huts were flooded and about 200 people came down with scurvy. The provisions were dwindling and there were no expert farmers to enable the community to become self-supporting. Phillip again went out in search of fertile land and then decided to form a settlement at what the natives called Parramatta which he named Rose Hill.

At the beginning of Phillip's second year in office food stocks were dwindling at an alarming rate. It was necessary to introduce strict measures to preserve the existing supply — convicts and marines were publicly hanged for plundering the stores. Food stocks were so low by October 1789, that the general ration was reduced by a third and by early 1790 the position was critical. Diarist Captain Watkin Tench wrote: '...gloom and dejection overspread every countenance'. The weekly rations were reduced even further to what was then 2½ lb of flour, 2 lb of rice and 2 lb of pork (2 lb is equal to about 100 grams less than 1 kilogram). The *Supply* was sent to Batavia with orders to buy food.

But in the meantime the situation further worsened with the arrival of 222 women convicts on the *Lady Juliana*. Fortunately the *Justinian* arrived two weeks later with supplies and full rations were thankfully restored. The Second Fleet arrived in June with 750 convicts and a detachment of 100 members of the New South Wales Corps, a unit recruited to take over garrison

107

duties from the marines. The Third Fleet arrived between July and October.

With even more mouths to feed, by early 1792 food stocks were again very low, and again the rations were reduced. Judge-Advocate Collins wrote: 'Distressing as it was to see the poor wretches dropping into the grave it was far more afflicting to observe the countenances and emaciated persons of many who remained soon to follow their miserable companions.'

The authorities in London, at last recognizing the dire effects of this food shortage sent assurance that in future there would be regular shipments of food and as first fulfilment of this pledge the *Britannia* arrived in Sydney on 26 July with good supplies.

ment in December 1792. Great changes then took place. The government of the colony passed into the hands of Major Francis Grose, commandant of the New South Wales Corps, and the order established by Governor Phillip rapidly disappeared. The officers of the 'Rum Corps', as they soon became known, had a completely free hand and built a stranglehold upon the community which three subsequent governors could not break. Extravagant land grants were made to the officers and they were allowed an excessive supply of convict labour, whom they paid with spirits instead of money. The military and civil officers eagerly seized the opportunity for making money by this trafficking and spirits were imported from all over the world. Drunken debauchery was rampant.

MacArthur's homestead, Camden

Even though these first years were marked by famine and hard times, several of the convicts were winning their way to prosperity. The most notable of these was John Irving who became the first convict to win emancipation for his 'unremitting good conduct' and was later to become assistant to Thomas Arndell, the senior surgeon at Parramatta. James Squire, after serving his sentence of seven years transportation, became the colony's first brewer. By 1820 his brewery was producing 40 hogshead of ale a week. The dubious distinction of New South Wales's first bushranger goes to a Negro from Madagascar, known as 'Black Caesar' who took to the bush and lived by plundering farms and huts on the outskirts of the settlement.

Phillip, for reasons of ill health, left the settle-

In 1795, the Home Office, aware of the loose state of the colony, appointed a new Governor — Captain John Hunter. He immediately struck trouble with the officers of the New South Wales Corps and was finally recalled in 1800. He was replaced by Philip Gidley King. When King arrived to 'sweep the colony clean' probably the most influential man in the community was John MacArthur, the unofficial leader of the Rum Corps.

MacArthur was a wealthy land holder, having 1610 acres (about 650 hectares) in his possession and a flock of imported merino and crossbred sheep. He was Grose's righthand man and responsible for most of the policy-making. King intensely disagreed with his methods, saying that there were 'no resources which art, cunning impudence and a pair of bailisk eyes can afford that he does not put into practice'. MacArthur was sent to England in 1801 to face a court martial and King was granted a respite to get on with the business of reforming the colony.

He succeeded in cutting down the consumption of alcohol — he sent 69 484 gallons (about 335 870 litres) of spirits and 31 293 gallons (about 142 290 litres) of wine back to England. Within a short time he had 300 convicts working government farms and had imported a large amount of live-stock from India. He encouraged experiments in growing hemp, indigo, cotton, vines and tobacco. Several public buildings were erected — an orphanage, churches, granary, brewery, wharves, mills and a bridge at Sydney. King also did much

During his time in office King had one major clash with the convicts. In 1802 a government farm was established at Castle Hill and 200 con-victs, mainly Irish, had been employed there. The Irish were, according to King, 'seditious people sent from Ireland since the late disturbances in that country'.

On 3 March 1804, there was an uprising at Castle Hill when the convicts overpowered the militia, seized their arms and headed for the Hawkesbury gathering recruits and more arms as they went. Martial law was declared and the militia called out in force. There was one con-frontation at Vinegar Hill and 15 men were killed and 26 captured. King issued a government order: 'If they don't give themselves up to the settle-

Old Government House, Parramatta

to encourage exploration. Under his administra-tion the first settlements were formed at Van Diemen's Land and Port Phillip and a penal sta-tion was opened at Newcastle. He actively assisted Matthew Flinders in his surveying and charting of the Australian coast.

However, the friction and thinly concealed hostility still existed between the Governor and the New South Wales Corps, the latter managing to convince the British Government that King was unfit for the job and he was recalled. To rub salt further into the wound, MacArthur made a glo-rious return to Sydney having resigned his com-mission and decided to return to the colony to develop the fine wool industry, with a government grant of 5000 acres (about 2025 hectares) of land.

ments and masters they respectively belong to . . . the most exemplary example will be made of them.' Most of the insurgents surrendered, the leaders were court-martialled and hanged.

Captain William Bligh arrived to replace King in August 1806. He had been warned that Mac-Arthur would be his strongest adversary and soon learned the truth of this. An eventual trial of strength between him and MacArthur was in-evitable. It came in October 1807 with the arrival of the *Dart*, a ship owned by MacArthur and which was carrying two large stills. Bligh had pre-viously issued a regulation against the importing of stills and the local distillation of spirits was strictly prohibited. Bligh ordered the stills to be im-pounded. There was much confusion which culminated in MacArthur bringing an action for illegal seizure.

The magistrates found in MacArthur's favour. Rejoicing, he accelerated his battle to get Bligh removed. Bligh retaliated by taking proceedings out against MacArthur for shipping a convict out of the colony on the *Parramatta*, one of MacArthur's vessels. MacArthur refused to be arrested, sending the man bearing the warrant away with a note that read '...I never will submit to the horrid tyranny that is attempted until I am forced... I consider it with scorn and contempt, as I do the persons who have directed the warrant to be executed.' The following day MacArthur was arrested in Sydney.

The general public was so incensed by MacArthur's imprisonment that an insurrection was imminent. Major Johnston of the New South Wales Corps, seizing the opportunity that this unrest afforded, assumed the title of Lieutenant-Governor and signed an order for MacArthur's release. Bligh was handed a letter relieving him of his command and Johnston proclaimed martial law.

For the next two years the colony was ruled by a corrupt rebel government, neglectful of public works and colonial administration. Nearly all Bligh's allies were deposed and their places taken by members of the New South Wales Corps. MacArthur was given a retrial, acquitted on all charges and appointed Secretary to the Colony. Bligh was confined to Government House and was powerless to do anything but write desperate letters decrying the rebel acts to the authorities in London. On 28 July 1808, Lieutenant-Colonel Joseph Foveaux, Johnston's senior officer, returned to the colony. But nothing changed.

Bligh eventually returned to England in 1810, after spending several months in Collin's Van Diemen's Land settlement futilely awaiting new orders from England. It was only when he had news of Governor Macquarie's arrival in New South Wales that he sailed for home.

Colonel Lachlan Macquarie brought with him an order recalling the New South Wales Corps to England. His other great advantage was that he was accompanied by his own regiment, the 73rd. He also arrived at an opportune time as most of the leaders of the rebellion against Bligh were on their way to England to explain their illegal act. Macquarie had been instructed to reinstate Bligh

as Governor for 24 hours before taking over from him, but as Bligh was in Van Diemen's Land this was impossible and Macquarie moved straight into office. His first proclamation expressed the King's 'high displeasure and disapprobation of the mutinous and outrageous conduct displayed in the forcible and unwarrantable removal of his late representative, William Bligh Esq., and of the tumultuous proceedings connected therewith'. All appointments, land grants, leases, pardons granted and sentences imposed by the rebel regime were revoked and all office-holders under Bligh's government were reinstated.

A daunting task lay before Macquarie. People were living in poverty, agriculture was neglected and public works were decaying. Macquarie encouraged settlers to grow more crops; church going and the marriage rate increased under his Calvinistic thoroughness, and the number of licensed public houses was reduced from 75 to 25. He embarked upon an extensive public works programme, realigning streets, building a market place, a new hospital, public storehouses and new convict and military barracks. Towards the end of 1810 he opened a new toll-road between Sydney and Parramatta.

He also did much to foster the leisure activities of the young colony, creating Hyde Park as an outdoor social centre and encouraging horse-racing and cricket. On Christmas Day 1810 St Phillip's Church was consecrated.

Macquarie had by then achieved a great deal. He had restored the people's morale and for the first time the colony had the appearance of stability and plenty.

Macquarie was not only content with reforming the settlements; he thirsted for the discovery of new pastoral lands and for the establishment of new towns. He set out on many expeditions to the surrounding countryside, inspecting existing farms and naming new towns such as Windsor, Richmond, Castlereagh and Wilberforce. It was during Macquarie's term in office that the elusive passage over the Blue Mountains was discovered by Gregory Blaxland, William Lawson and William Charles Wentworth. Now that the interior was accessible progress was rapid.

Macquarie sent his surveyor, George Evans, to follow the explorers' path over the Great Dividing Range. Evans travelled more than 158 km beyond Mt Blaxland and on his return reported that '12

Sydney Heads, from the south

111

men might clear a good road in three months for a cart to travel over the mountains and make the descent of them so easy that it might be drove down in safety'. By March 1815 the road to Bathurst Plains had been completed. In 1817 and 1818 John Oxley investigated the middle reaches of the Macquarie River and on his return journey discovered the fine country of the Liverpool Plains and New England Tablelands.

During Macquarie's time in office great debate was surrounding the question whether New South Wales should remain a penal settlement or not. The convicts who had served their time were now living as free settlers and were involved in farming, trading and public office. Meanwhile the convict settlements at Newcastle and Macquarie Harbour continued with single-mindedness. The incorrigible prisoners were sent to these settlements and for years Macquarie Harbour was the most dreaded penal station in Australia. Macquarie did much to encourage the emancipist prisoners and his attitude towards them was partly the reason for Britain's decision in 1819 to appoint John Thomas Bigge as Commissioner of Inquiry into New South Wales and to send him to report on the colony.

Bigge believed that New South Wales' future lay in the development of fine wool. The colony's expenditure had to be reduced and therefore public works had to be reduced. He suggested that the best employment for the convicts would be working for the government in clearing the land for the free settlers from England or that they should be assigned to the large landholders who wanted to graze sheep and cattle west of the Blue Mountains.

In 1822 Macquarie completed his term of office and sailed home. A year later, acting on Bigge's suggestions the Colonial Office framed a Bill 'for the better administration of justice in New South Wales'. Before 1822 the administration of the transportation system was unreliable and expensive. Most of Bigge's suggestions for economy and severity, land grants and assignment were to be implemented by Governors Brisbane and Darling by 1831.

When he left New South Wales, Macquarie said 'I found New South Wales a jail and left it a colony. I found a population of idle prisoners, paupers and paid officials and left a large free community thriving in the produce of flocks and the labour of convicts.'

Still the question remained. Was the colony to be an open prison or was it to have the status of a free society? The new Governor, Sir Thomas Brisbane, entered a very turbulent and factious society. The first major reform he attempted was to do with land tenure. Settlers had moved out into all remote areas and boundaries were ill-defined. The squatters owned land by the rule of possession. The people who had been promised land grants found this particularly frustrating. To overcome this, Brisbane issued 'tickets of occupation' which enabled holders to occupy the land before it had been surveyed. The land could not be legally claimed until it had been surveyed and a grant had been issued.

The result was the opening up of thousands of hectares of land that would previously have been either illegally occupied or not occupied at all. Brisbane also instituted the rule that for every hundred acres of land granted to a settler that settler was required to take and maintain one convict — thus reducing government expense. His other important move was to make land available for sale, as a means of raising revenue. In July 1824 he announced that land would be available at 5/– an acre (about 0.4 hectare) and 18 months later 334 000 acres (about 135 200 hectares) had been contracted to be sold. The availability of land and convict labour to make improvements upon that land soon opened up the colony.

There was remarkable progress during Brisbane's administration. In 1823, Britain passed an Act which conferred an advisory Legislative Council and Supreme Court on New South Wales. Immigration greatly increased during these years: in 1821 there were less than 30 000 people, in 1825 the population had increased to over 36 000. The immigrants were mainly men with considerable capital to invest in their land grants and the production and revenue of the colony accordingly escalated. Brisbane was recalled in 1825 and in his departing speech declared his support for the emancipists by saying the colony was ready for an elected legislature as well as for trial by jury.

Brisbane was replaced by Lieutenant-General Ralph Darling, who was also faced with the problem that the colony that had begun as a jail also had a large population of free settlers. The 1828 census showed that of the 36 598 white persons in New South Wales, 20 930 were free and 15 668 were convicts. By this year roughly 3500 people over the age of 12 years had been born in the colony.

Shipping, Circular Quay

The colony was changing and changes in administration had to be made to go with it. An Executive Council was set up, similar to a Senate. The Colonial Office also changed the land policy — sales were encouraged and grants discouraged. People wanting grants were required to wait until 'the expiration of six months next after the time when any lands have been so offered for sale' before applying for their grants. This system of selling off land to the rich became the rallying point for a growing number of opponents to the government.

In the Act of 1828 the British Government recognized the changes that were taking place in New South Wales; the emerging 'squatter classes' that were clashing with the land owners, and the weaknesses that were becoming inherent in the existing form of government. The Act admitted

113

that New South Wales would eventually receive some form of administrative government. However, Darling was inflexible; 'No colony as long as it continues to be a receptacle for criminals can . . . be considered eligible to the possession of the English constitution.' Under the combined attacks of several political radicals in England, the Secretary of State advised Darling that he would be recalled at the end of his term.

In 1831, Major-General Richard Bourke became Governor of New South Wales. By now there was a deep social rift between the emancipists and those who had come to the colony as free settlers, but during the six years that Bourke administered the affairs of New South Wales, the colony was free from class warfare. Industry and commerce enjoyed rapid growth, and the aspirations of the liberals for the constitutional rights of free men first began to be realized. Trial by jury was granted in 1833 and, although representative government was still withheld by the Home Government, the administration of public affairs was conducted by Bourke on constitutional principles with very little resort to the arbitrary power that had made Darling's term unpopular. Assisted free immigration began in 1832, financed by the sale of colonial land.

Bourke left New South Wales in 1837 and was replaced by Governor Gipps who was immediately faced with a depression. The origins of the slump lay mainly within the colony itself, but the trends were reinforced by the fact that investors in Britain, hearing of the colony's difficulties, stopped investing their capital and attempted to recover their earlier investments. Incomes and prices fell, bankruptcy and unemployment rose, and the Bank of Australia fell.

Gipps attributed the depression to the preceding speculation and great influx of capital which had caused credit to be extended too liberally during the boom period. Gradually, in 1844, a degree of stability returned to the economy — the depression was allowed to work itself out.

At the same time as the depression there was trouble between the Crown and the squatters. Gipps was determined to secure as high a price as possible in selling Crown land. He restricted the amount of land to be put up for sale and increased the price in 1842 to £1 per acre. The economic depression had decreased the revenue from the sale of Crown land. As this revenue was the tradi-

Hunter Street, Newcastle

tional source for assisting immigration it looked as though immigration would dry up completely.

Gipps attempted to remedy this lack of revenue by issuing two sets of regulations: the Occupation Regulations whereby a separate licence was to be issued to each station of an area of 20 square miles, and the Purchase Regulation which proposed that every squatter after five years' occupation should be given the opportunity to buy at least 320 acres of his run. Despite the fairness of these regulations they were met with a storm of public protest.

The idea of obligatory purchase of homesteads was dropped. The outcome of the whole struggle was that squatters gained long leases and acquired a vested interest in maintaining a high minimum price for Crown Land as a guarantee of their continued occupation of squatting runs at low rents. This soon led to all squatting lands being virtually locked up in the hands of less than a thousand graziers. Gipps' land policy had been wrecked and there was still no acceptable compromise between the rights of the squatters and the rest of the community.

Transportation of convicts to New South Wales was abolished. To this time, a total of about 80 000 convicts had been transported to the colony. In 1843, a Legislative Council — consisting of one-third Crown nominees and two-thirds elected members — was introduced and brought the principle of popular representation partly into existence.

Sir George Gipps left New South Wales in 1846 and the new Governor, Sir Charles FitzRoy, began his administration at a time that heralded an era of prosperity.

The discovery of gold on the western slopes of the mountains in 1851 brought tens of thousands of immigrants into the country. On 12 February 1851, Edward Hargraves found gold at Radigan's Gully and a steady stream of gold-seekers began heading for Ophir. The great Australian gold rush had begun. The *Sydney Morning Herald* reported: 'From the intelligence received from Bathurst it appears that the Colony is to be cursed with gold diggings.' The New South Wales gold rush attracted 10 000 eager men before it tapered off and the rush switched to Ballarat and Bendigo in Victoria. The squatters were aghast as their shepherds deserted the farms and headed for the fields.

Governor FitzRoy at once issued a proclamation which declared that 'all mines of gold and all gold in its natural place of deposit... belong to the Crown', and warned that 'all persons who shall take from any lands within the said Territory, any gold metal or ore containing gold, or who within

Ocean Beach, Manly

any of the Wastelands which have not yet been alienated by the Crown, shall dig for and disturb the soil in search for such gold metal or ore without having been duly authorised in that behalf by Her Majesty's Colonial Government, shall be prosecuted, both Criminally and Civilly, as the law allows.'

But it was to no avail. 'The people are perfectly mad and are flocking in their hundreds to the land of Ophir,' wrote one squatter. Control was needed, and so FitzRoy introduced the mounted police and also a licence fee of 30/– a month, which was payable by each miner. The first shipment of gold from Sydney to London was estimated to be worth between £800 to £1000. A month later the amount transported was valued at £10 000 a week.

With the discovery of gold, FitzRoy's administration was a prosperous one, giving a boost to the decades ahead. The colony passed through an extraordinary time of progress: a satisfactory constitutional settlement was reached; the transportation of convicts was completely abolished; land squatting became an orderly system with the Robertson Land Reform Acts of 1861 when unsurveyed land could be purchased by free selectors and the terms of the squatters' leases were reduced; railways were introduced; a steam postal service began operating between the colony and Britain; and a national system of education was begun. Large-scale irrigation systems opened up vast tracts of ground and farming became highly productive. Banks became more speculative and began buying and selling land. Also overseas markets for primary produce were found.

However in the 1880s the overseas price for wool fell dramatically. Loans from abroad were withdrawn, banks fell and bankruptcy became common. After a long hard period the banks were brought under Government control and paper money was issued instead of gold. Prosperity slowly returned.

New South Wales, which had been given self-government in 1850, with the other colonies voted for Federation in 1900.

Places of interest

NEW SOUTH WALES

Sydney and environs

Agar Steps,
 The Rocks
Anzac War Memorial,
 Hyde Park,
 Sydney
Archibald Fountain,
 Hyde Park,
 Sydney
Argyle Centre,
 Argyle Street,
 Sydney
Argyle Place,
 The Rocks,
 Sydney
Art Gallery of New South Wales,
 Art Gallery Road,
 Domain,
 Sydney
Australian Museum,
 6 College Street,
 Sydney

Barrenjoey Lighthouse,
 Palm Beach
Bondi Beach
Botanic Gardens, Royal,
 Macquarie Street,
 Sydney

Cadman's Cottage,
 110 George Street,
 Sydney
Captain Cook's Landing Place,
 Kurnell
Cenotaph,
 Martin Place,
 Sydney
Central Railway Station
Circular Quay Plaza
Conservatorium of Music,
 Macquarie Street,
 Sydney

Customs House,
 Circular Quay,
 Sydney

Domain, The

El Alamein Fountain,
 Kings Cross
Elizabeth Bay House — colonial restoration,
 7 Onslow Avenue,
 Elizabeth Bay
Elizabeth Farm House, Parramatta
Ervin Museum and Art Gallery,
 Observatory Hill,
 Sydney
Experiment Farm Cottage,
 9 Ruse Street
 Parramatta

Fort Denison ('Pinchgut'),
 Sydney Harbour

Garden Island
Garrison Church (Holy Trinity),
 Lower Fort Street,
 Millers Point
General Post Office,
 Martin Place,
 Sydney
Government House,
 Macquarie Street,
 Sydney
Great Synagogue,
 160 Castlereagh Street,
 Sydney

Harbour Bridge
Hero of Waterloo Hotel,
 81 Lower Fort Street,
 Millers Point
Holy Trinity Church (Garrison Church),
 Lower Fort Street,
 Millers Point
Hyde Park
Hyde Park Barracks (Law Courts),
 Queens Square
 Sydney

Kings Cross
Ku-ring-gai Chase National Park

Lancer Barracks,
   Smith Street,
   Parramatta
Law Courts,
   Queens Square,
   Sydney
Library of New South Wales,
   Macquarie Street,
   Sydney
'Lindesay' — colonial restoration,
   Carthona Avenue,
   Darling Point

Macquarie Place
Macquarie University,
   Balaclava Road,
   North Ryde
Manly
Martin Plaza
Mining Museum
   36 George Street,
   Sydney
Mitchell Library,
   Macquarie Street,
   Sydney
Mrs Macquarie's Chair,
   Royal Botanic Gardens,
   Sydney
Museum of Applied Arts and Sciences,
   659 Harris Street,
   Ultimo

National Park, Royal
National Trust,
   Observatory Hill,
   Sydney
Northern Beaches

Observatory,
   Observatory Park,
   Watson Road,
   Millers Point
Old Customs House,
   Circular Quay,
   Sydney
Old Government House,
   Parramatta Park,
   Parramatta
Old Mint Building,
   Macquarie Street,
   Sydney
Opera House,
   Bennelong Point,
   Sydney

Palm Beach
Parliament House,
   Macquarie Street, Sydney
'Pinchgut' (Fort Denison),
   Sydney Harbour

Queen Victoria Building,
   George Street,
   Sydney

Randwick Racecourse,
   Randwick
Richmond Villa — historic house,
   120 Kent Street,
   Sydney
Royal National Park

St Andrew's Cathedral,
   Sydney Square,
   Sydney
St James' Church,
   King Street,
   Sydney
St John's Church,
   Church Street,
   Parramatta
St Mary's Cathedral,
   College Street,
   Sydney
St Philip's Church,
   York Street,
   Sydney
St Stephen's Church,
   197 Macquarie Street,
   Sydney
Southern Beaches
State Library of New South Wales,
   Macquarie Street,
   Sydney
Sydney Hospital,
   Macquarie Street,
   Sydney

Taronga Zoo Park
The Domain,
   Sydney
The Rocks,
   Sydney
Town Hall,
   Sydney Square,
   Sydney

University of New South Wales,
   Anzac Parade,
   Kensington
University of Sydney,
   Parramatta Road,
   Newtown

Vaucluse House,
    Wentworth Road,
    Vaucluse
Victoria Barracks,
    Moore Park Road,
    Paddington

West Head

Zoological Park, Taronga

Beyond Sydney

Abercombie Caves
Armidale University,
    Armidale
Australian Village,
    Wilberforce

Barrington Tops National Park
Ben Boyd National Park
Berrima Gaol,
    Berrima
Blue Mountains
Bouddi National Park
Brisbane Water National Park
Burragorang, Lake
Burrendong Dam

Camden Park Homestead — historic house,
    Camden

Dharug National Park
Dorrigo State Park

Gibraltar Range National Park

Hartley — historic township
Hill End — historic township
Hunter Valley — vineyards and wineries

Jenolan Caves

Kanchega National Park
Karingal Village, near Bathurst
Kosciusko National Park

Lachlan Vintage Village,
    Forbes
Lake Burragorang
Lake Eucumbene
Lake Macquarie
Lightning Ridge Opal Fields
Lord Howe Island

Menindee Lakes
Mootwingee Historic Site
Morton National Park
Mount Canobolas, Orange
Mount Kaputar National Park

Murrumbidgee Irrigation Area
Myall Lakes National Park

New England National Park
New England University, Armidale

'Old Sydney Town' — historic re-creation,
    near Gosford
Overseas Telecommunications Station, Moree

Radio Telescope, Parkes
Richmond RAAF Base,

St Matthew's Church,
    Windsor
Snowy River Hydro-electric Scheme
Southern Highlands
Sturt National Park
Surveyor-General Inn — historic house,
    Berrima

'Timbertown', near Wauchope

Warrumbungle National Park
Wellington Caves
Western Plains Zoo, Dubbo
Wineries and vineyards — Griffith, Hunter Valley,
    Mudgee, Wellington
Wombeyan Caves

Yarrangobilly Caves

AUSTRALIAN CAPITAL TERRITORY

Academy of Science,
    Gordon Street,
    City
Australian-American Memorial,
    Russell Drive,
    Canberra
Australian National Gallery,
    14 Molonglo Mall,
    Fyshwick
Australian National University,
    Canberra
Australian War Memorial,
    Anzac Parade,
    Canberra

Canberra City — Australian National Capital
Captain Cook Memorial,
    Lake Burley Griffin
Carillon,
    Aspen Island,
    Lake Burley Griffin
Cotter Dam

Duntroon Military College,
Duntroon

Government House,
Dunrossil Drive,
Yarralumla

High Court of Australia,
King Edward Terrace,
Parkes

Lake Burley Griffin

Mount Ainslie
Mount Stromlo Observatory

National Library,
Parkes Place,
Canberra

Parliament House,
King George Terrace,
Canberra

Red Hill Lookout
Royal Australian Mint,
Deakin

St John's Church,
Constitution Avenue,
Reid
Space Tracking Stations — Honeysuckle Creek,
Tidbinbilla

Telecommunications Tower, Black Mountain
Tidbinbilla Nature Reserve

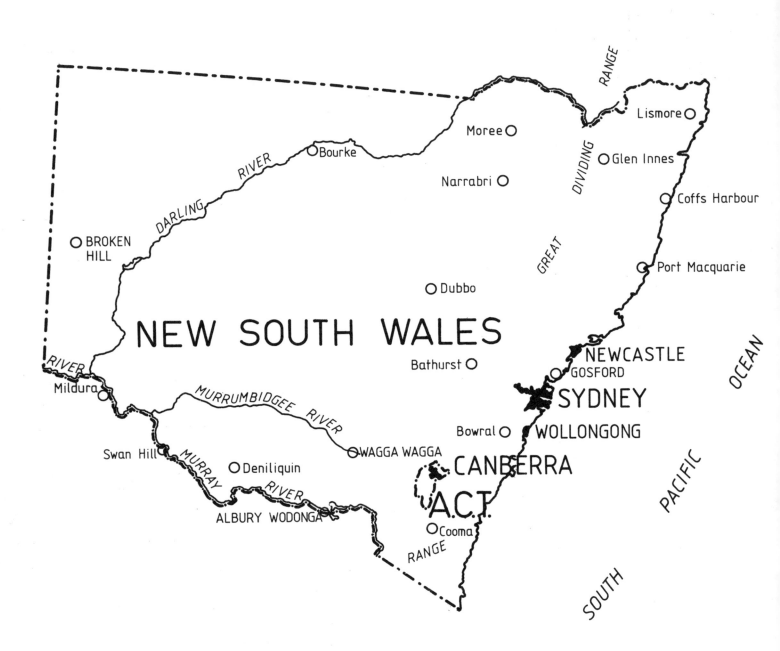

Argyle Place in the historical rocks area, Sydney.
Despite the intrusions of modern man and with the assistance of a restoration program, The Rocks has managed to preserve its atmos- *phere. It gives a potted history of Sydney since its inception almost two centuries ago. (Higgins)*

Restored and in operation in The Rocks district, this postbox is a relic of the Victorian era. (Higgins)

Sydney's Opera House — the city's centre of the performing arts — beside the harbour on Bennelong Point.

The Royal Viking Star *at majestic rest in Sydney Harbour. (Higgins)*

Sydney's most distinctive landmarks: the soaring sails of the Opera House and the splendid arch of the Harbour Bridge. (Higgins)

Chinese Gardens at the new entertainment development at Darling Harbour, Sydney. (Higgins)

The famous Sydney Opera House on Bennelong Point. (Higgins)

Martin Place, Sydney. The flower-seller and his flowers brighten this busy pedestrian plaza. (Higgins)

Meditation and remembrance in Martin Place, focal point for Sydney's ceremony and celebration. Each Thursday a short ceremony marks the changing of the Cenotaph guards. (Dawes)

People spill through the Sydney streets in rivers at the start of the City to Surf race. (Higgins)

Doyles on the Beach restaurant at Watsons Bay. (Higgins)

Victorian-style terrace houses perch on the hills of Paddington. Built in the 1870s, these charming houses are being tastefully restored and Paddington has become one of Sydney's most fashionable inner suburbs. (Dawes)

Old Government House, Parramatta — the oldest public building in Australia. Designed for Governor Macquarie and completed in 1816, the building was leased to the Kings School as a boarding school in 1910. After complete renovation by the National Trust the building was opened to the public in 1970. (Dawes)

Physical and cultural combine at the Art Gallery of New South Wales in the Sydney Domain. The building, an incongruous mix of classic columns and modern materials, houses a stunning collection of Melanesian and Aboriginal art. (Dawes)

The Government Windmill, shortly before its completion, at Old Sydney Town, an authentic reconstruction of Sydney Cove and the surrounding settlement as it existed between 1788 and 1810. (Solness)

◁ The Kurnell Oil Refinery shows a smoky silhouette to surf-board riders at Cronulla — Sydney's most popular southern beach. (Solness)

△
Beaches are the village green of Sydney's summer social life. Manly is a favourite surf beach on the northern side of the city. (Higgins)

Kayaks are becoming popular on all Sydney's northern beaches. (Higgins)

The Three Sisters, an extraordinary rock formation at Echo Point near Katoomba in the Blue Mountains National Park. (Dawes)

Autumn at the town of Mt Wilson in the Blue Mountains. (Higgins)

Sheer cliffs of the Kanangra Walls in the Blue Mountains. On a clear day one can see Sydney's Harbour Bridge — more than 100 kilometres away — from this vantage point. (Higgins)

The start of the Bridge to Bridge Race along the Hawkesbury. Here seen at Dangar Island. (Higgins)

The forlorn ruin of MacDonald Valley Inn near Wisemans Ferry. (Higgins)

Sunset at Long Neck Lagoon reserve near Cattai on Wisemans Ferry Road. (Higgins)

Bushells Lagoon, Wilberforce. The lagoon dried out during a recent drought — the second time in recorded history that it has ever done so. (Higgins)

The Nepean River at Penrith is a popular area for speed boats and canoeists. The annual 100-mile (about 160 kilometres) canoe race is held here. (Higgins)

The Macquarie River, near Hill End, a popular place for weekend campers. ▷▷ (Higgins)

Established in 1894, Ku-ring-gai Chase National Park is the home of a wide range of birdlife, including the cheeky kookaburra. (Dawes)

Formerly a bustling gold mining town with a population of 30 000 and 52 hotels, the now sleepy Hill End has been proclaimed a national historic village. The Royal Hotel is the only hotel still standing. (Higgins, Dawes)

Golden Gully, Hill End. The huge Beyers and Holtermann nugget was found in this area in 1872. (Higgins)

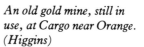

The famous historic village of Carcoar — scene of New South Wales' first bank hold-up in 1863. (Wigney)

An old gold mine, still in use, at Cargo near Orange. (Higgins)

The former gold mining town of Newnes on the Wolgan River. (Higgins)

Parkes, first settled in 1862 when gold was discovered, is now the commercial and industrial centre for the surrounding agricultural area. (Wigney)

Sheep grazing on the outskirts of the former gold-mining town of Forbes. It was somewhere near here that Ben Hall, the famous bushranger, was gunned down by police in 1865. He is buried in the Forbes cemetery. (Wigney)

Australia's greatest open range wildlife park — the Western Plains Zoo, 5 kilometres south-west of Dubbo. Animals from six continents roam freely over the countryside. (Wigney)

Warrumbungle National Park contains some of the most spectacular scenery in Australia. Aboriginal for 'broken mountains', the Warrumbungle Ranges comprise deep gorges and precipitous rock faces — a mountaineer's paradise. (Higgins)

The Breadknife — a gargantuan, 90 metre high sliver of rock in the Warrumbungle Ranges. (Higgins)

Golden wildflowers, at Lake Cargelligo. This small township surrounds a lake sanctuary, home of many bird species including pelicans, galahs and, at times, the rare black cockatoo. (Higgins)

The picturesque Lachlan River flowing through Hillston (far right, below) and Condoblin (far right, above). (Higgins)

△
Rolling sand dunes near Wentworth. (Higgins)

◁ *The Lake Mungo area of western New South Wales — once a lush tropical lake area — contains some
of the oldest recordings known of man. (Higgins)*

Silverton Gaol and Historical Museum. Silver chlorides were discovered at Silverton in 1883. Six years later the field closed and the miners made for Broken Hill. (Higgins)

Canoes have replaced paddle steamers on the Darling River at Wilcannia, once a key inland port. (Andrews)

Wheat silos in western New South Wales. Australia is one of the world's top grain producers and exporters, with wheat being grown in all States except Tasmania. (Higgins)

The Tasman crashes onto ▷
the coast of New South
Wales in glistening
breakers. (Solness)

Cape Byron, the most
easterly point of the Aus-
tralian mainland. (Dawes)

The bluff, Tenterfield.
(Higgins)

UFF CREEK

Fishing and prawn fleets are based at Maclean on the delta of the Clarence River. About twenty per cent of New South Wales' seafood is netted by fishermen from here and the nearby towns of Yamba and Iluka. (Solness)

△
Gibraltar Range National Park, east of Glen ▷ Innes, is an area of lush rainforest noted for its wildflowers and wildlife. (Higgins)

Overleaf: Rich dairylands border the Bellinger River on the north coast of New South Wales. (Andrews)

The huge concrete 'Big Banana' (below) at
Coffs Harbour is a symbol of the surrounding
banana plantations (left). Visitors may enter the
banana and view displays illustrating the
banana industry. (Higgins)

Jacaranda trees lining the wide streets of
Grafton. A glorious Jacaranda Festival is held
annually in November. (Wigney)

Sawtell is a quiet beach near the busy city of Coffs Harbour. (Higgins)

Autumn tones at the attractive tourist city of Armidale in the New England Ranges. (Higgins)

'Booloominbah' mansion, now administration centre for the University of New England, Armidale. (Higgins)

Trial Bay Gaol near Kempsey. The building, with walls 5.5 m high and 45 cm thick, took its first complement of prisoners in 1886. The gaol was closed in 1903, although it was used again during World War I to confine German internees. (Higgins)

A re-creation of the story of Snow White and the Seven Dwarfs at Fantasy Glades, Port Macquarie. (Higgins)

Pebbly Beach, Forster. (Wigney)

The Myall River at the delightful town of Tea Gardens, near Port Stephens. (Higgins)

Myall Lakes National Park, 12 kilometres east of Bulahdelah, has spectacular headlands, long expanses of beach and over 1000 hectares of lakes. (Higgins)

Some of the hand-crafted toys at Sugar Creek Toymakers, a great tourist attraction at Smiths Lake. (Higgins)

Dutchmans Bay at Port Stephens. This large deepwater port has a
harbour two-and-a-half times the size of Sydney Harbour.
(Wigney)

The Customs House at Newcastle, the seventh largest city
in Australia and one of the country's most important centres for the
manufacture of steel and steel products. Its port is the clearing point
for northern New South Wales' coalfields. (Wigney)

Rural scene in the Hunter Valley, one of the most important wine
growing areas in Australia. (Higgins)

Stockton Bridge, Newcastle. (Higgins)

Newcastle Mall. (Higgins)

Surf Rescue Team, Newcastle. (Higgins)

Mangrove trees line the Hunter River at Newcastle. (Higgins)

Sunset on Lake Macquarie, the largest seaboard lake in Australia. (Higgins)

Catamarans at Belmont, one of the main resorts on the beautiful Lake Macquarie. (Higgins)

Night reflections at the Belmont Yacht Club. (Higgins)

Massed colour at the Tulip Festival held every October in Bowral. (Green)

Spray reaches up to welcome a rainbow at Kiama, south of Sydney. (Dawes)

Fitzroy Falls tumble through rainforest in Morton National Park. (Higgins)

Fishing boats at Jervis Bay. In 1915 jurisdiction of this fine natural port was transferred from New South Wales to the Australian Capital Territory to give the Federal Capital sea access. (Higgins)

South coast seascapes. (Higgins)△▷

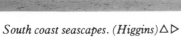
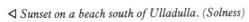

◁ *Sunset on a beach south of Ulladulla. (Solness)*

New Parliament House on Capital Hill, Canberra, was opened by HRH Queen Elizabeth II in our Bicentennial year. (Hermes)

The heart of Canberra — Old Parliament House. The low, white building was opened by the Duke and Duchess of York in 1927. (Dawes)

Visitors gather outside New Parliament House to inspect this spectacular building. (Hermes)

The large saucer-shaped antenna of the Tidbinbilla tracking station in a lonely valley 40 kilometres from Canberra. The centre receives information from spacecraft exploring the far reaches of the solar system and is one of three such stations in the Australian Capital Territory. (Higgins)

Overleaf: A model within a model city — Cockington Green, Canberra. (Dawes)

Vineyards at Griffith. Developed as a model settlement, the town was planned by Walter Burley Griffin, the architect of Canberra. (Green)

Trees stand helpless against the dark sky of an approaching storm near Tumut. (Higgins)

Snowfields at Perisher and Smiggin Holes within the Kosciusko National Park are a magnet to skiers throughout Australia. The snow sports season usually starts in late May and continues until mid or late October. (Higgins)

◁ *Downhill skiers, Kosciusko National Park. (Higgins)*

Lake Jindabyne, Snowy Mountains. (Wigney)

The Avenue of Flags, Centennial Park, Cooma. The flags of 27 countries were unfurled here in 1959 to commemorate the 10th

anniversary of the Snowy Mountains Hydro-Electric Authority. Cooma was once dubbed Australia's most cosmopolitan town when thousands of migrants came here to work on the Snowy Mountains Scheme. (Wigney)

Bega, the centre of a rich dairying, mixed farming and pastoral district is well known for its output of high quality cheese. (Solness)

The Pinnacles at Ben Boyd National Park, near Eden. (Higgins)

Bridge over the Murray near Hume Weir — a man-made inland lake ideal for water sports. (Solness)

Lake Victoria. (Green)

Victoria and Tasmania

W. HATHERELL.

Victoria

THE first sighting of the eastern coast of Australia was in 1770, when Lieutenant Hicks in Captain James Cook's *Endeavour* sighted the Victorian coast at the place now known as Cape Everard.

When the convict colony had been established at Botany Bay in 1788 the territory which is now Victoria had been placed under the Governor of New South Wales and the land south of the Murray was considered a separate region known as the Southern District. The area had not been officially explored by white men and it was not until 1797-8 when George Bass and Matthew Flinders surveyed the coast at closer quarters that the strait between Van Diemen's Land and the mainland was discovered.

In 1802 Lieutenant John Murray discovered Port Phillip Bay and in the following year Philip King, governor of New South Wales, sent his Surveyor-General, Charles Grimes, to investigate the area discovered by Murray with the view of establishing another penal colony. Grimes made a detailed record of the area and found 'a great river mouth', the estuary of the Yarra River.

Six months later David Collins began a penal colony at Sorrento. 'The disadvantages of Port Phillip and the unsuitability of the "bay" itself when viewed in a commercial light for the purposes of colonial establishment' were strongly dwelt upon by Collins in his despatches to the Admiralty and he ventured to predict that the harbour would never be 'resorted to by speculative men'. Collins abandoned this venture a year later and he and his party moved on to settle the Derwent area in Van Diemen's Land.

The governors of New South Wales ignored Port Phillip for the next twenty-five years, generally believing that the area was unsuitable for colonization. But the area held possibilities for the free settler graziers in Van Diemen's Land who were aware that they would need more land to supply the island's penal colonies with fresh meat and other essential produce. Parties from Van Diemen's Land explored the south coast of the mainland and the first permanent settlement in Victoria was established by a little colony of Englishmen — the brothers Henty — who landed in Portland Bay in 1834 with farm servants, livestock, agricultural implements and stores and became the pioneers of the great pastoral industry of Victoria.

Hume and Hovell's exploration of the region in 1824 led to increased interest and several syndicates were established to appeal to the government to grant land leases in Port Phillip area but these applications were curtly dismissed by the masters in Sydney. The most adamant of these syndicates was the Port Phillip association, which consisted of John Batman, J. T. Gellibrand, J. H. Wedge, and 12 other members who were mainly officials attracted by financial speculation. After battling to get government approval, the syndicate finally chose to ignore the legalities and agreed to finance an unofficial expedition to look for grazing land in

Thomas Henty

John Batman treating with the Aborigines

Port Phillip. Each financial member was to receive the right to an equal share in any suitable land that might be discovered.

On 28 May 1835, Batman landed at Port Phillip Bay and organized an expedition into the surrounding countryside, which he found to have black, rich earth. 'I never saw anything to equal the land in my life,' he wrote. On 8 June Batman 'purchased' about 600 000 acres (273 000 hectares) of land from natives of the Doutagalla tribe for an annual tribute of trade goods worth about £100. The exchange ceremony was simple but impressive — the Aborigines cut their totem on the bark of a tree and Batman copied this as signatures on the Deeds of Conveyance; 400 lb of blankets, tomahawks, knives, looking-glasses, handkerchiefs, shirts and flour were handed over and the Aborigines passed Batman a handful of soil as a symbol of handing over ownership of the land.

Batman headed south-west and stumbled upon the Yarra. His journal prophetically read, 'The boat went up the large river I have spoken about

and, I am glad to state, about six miles up found the river all good water and very deep. This will be the place for a village.' The site was to become Melbourne. He sailed back to Launceston and on 7 August, with surveyor Wedge, Henry Batman, and his family he sailed for Indented Head on the Bellarine Peninsula to establish a settlement.

Another Launceston free settler, John Pascoe Fawkner, was also intent on acquiring land in Victoria. On 27 July 1835 a party of self-styled 'independents' sailed for Westernport. Fawkner didn't make the journey but Captain John Lancey, master in command, discovered grassland some distance up the Yarra River after rejecting the poor land around Westernport.

Lancey wrote to Fawkner: 'A more delightful spot, I think, cannot be. Beautiful trees, a pleasant prospect, a fine freshwater river and the vessel lying alongside the bank discharging at a musket shot distance from a pleasant hill, where I intend to put your house.' Lancey established camp and began a settlement.

John Pascoe Faulkner

Times were initially hard for these pioneers. Lack of suitable materials hindered building, timber had to be imported from the other colonies, but the rich growing lands and favourable climate spurred the settlers on. The most important difficulty was the question of the settlement's legal status. Relationships with the Aborigines were becoming a serious problem in the surrounding countryside and it was evident that a ruling authority was needed to arbitrate and to avert the outbreak of serious violence. So the colonists agreed to petition Governor Bourke in New South Wales for a police magistrate.

The British Authorities finally recognized that it would be impracticable to evict these 'trespassing' settlers and consequently sanctioned the settlement in April 1836. George Stewart, police magistrate at Goulburn was sent to report on the situation at Port Phillip. Batman's Deed with the Aborigines was not officially recognized but the Government paid him £7000 compensation for colonization expenses.

Port Phillip district developed rapidly as a squatting colony and by 1837 the white population had grown to around 500. Fawkner played a large part in the growth of this settlement. He initiated a farmers' co-operative society whereby funds were raised to enable the society to buy land at public auction so that shareholders who wished to take up farms at a later date avoided the inflationary prices of land speculators.

Captain William Lonsdale was appointed by Governor Darling in 1836 to administer the Port Phillip settlement. With the help of surveyors Robert Russell and Robert Hoddle, the town was planned. Hoddle convinced the Governor of the convenience of streets 99 ft (about 30 m) wide and the Governor suggested the addition of narrow lanes as 'mews or approaches to the stablings and outbuildings of the main streets of buildings'. Governor Bourke later visited the new town and named it Melbourne after the British Prime Minister. Williamstown and Geelong were also planned and laid out, the former being named after the ruling King.

Bourke despatched a report to Lord Glenelg in London recommending the appointment of a superintendent but not of a separate Legislative Council. Glenelg replied, directing that the profits from the land sales be poured back into the new community 'especially in the introduction of the free immigrants there who would supply the labour without the use of convicts'.

The land boom began. The first auction was held on 1 June 1837 when half-acre (about 0.2 ha) town allotments fetched between £18 and £95 with an average of £38. Auctions for the Victorian land were also held in Sydney and the field was wide open for speculation. Assisted immigrants arrived in Melbourne; banks were established with English backing and speculation reached magic proportions. The growth was phenomenal; the population of 500 in 1836 had swelled to 6000 by 1841.

The occupation of the Port Phillip district has been described as 'the most remarkable colonization feat in the annals of the British Empire'. Within five years all the area worth occupying had been occupied by pastoralists. The population increase, however did have its disadvantages in that public works could not keep pace, and New South Wales was reputedly very miserly in allocating funds for such works as public sewerage systems.

In 1839 Charles Joseph LaTrobe was appointed Superintendent of the district of Port Phillip — an office carrying the authority and function of a Lieutenant-Governor. He disembarked to find an evil smelling village with a high death rate and filthy streets. There was no drainage or sewerage, the buildings were ramshackle and the roads had been encroached upon by nature. Despite Port Phillip's six representatives on the Legislative

On the Yarra River

arrived in Melbourne with a load of convicts in 1849. The anger was so great that La Trobe ordered the ship straight on to Sydney. The British Government was forced to realize that the days of transportation were over for the eastern colonies.

The movement for separation was equally vehement. Throughout the 1840s Port Phillip pleaded for independence against continuous opposition from New South Wales.

As the community slowly emerged from the depression the call for funds from Sydney for public works became louder. The population was incensed when the New South Wales Government chose to spend £25 000 or erecting a solid blue-stone jail in Russell Street instead of spending the money on the much needed public buildings.

In 1844, Dr J. D. Lang, who was later to play an important part in the Queensland separatist movement, moved in the New South Wales Council that speedy steps would be taken for the separation of the Port Phillip district and its elevation to the status of an independent colony. He pointed out that the dependency of the 25 000 colonists had not cost England a penny and it was

Governor La Trobe

Council in New South Wales, adequate funds were still not forthcoming.

But even so some important and far-sighted projects began. The great public library was started, the University of Melbourne was projected, Melbourne Hospital was founded, and in 1846 the Botanical Gardens were begun under Ferdinand Von Mueller.

During the depression, jobs were scarce, but the community struggled through. The remarkably stable and prosperous years after 1846 were due to the ever-increasing wool-clip and the rising prices of wool.

The two unifying elements of the community during these years were the movements for separation and against transportation. Seventeen thousand 'reformed' prisoners from Pentonville jail worked on the land in the Port Phillip district between 1844 and 1847. There were objections to this but the adamant refusal to welcome convicts in this area reached its height when the *Randolph*

grossly unjust to bind them to New South Wales against their will. Lang's motion was defeated and he urged the separatists to petition Queen Victoria. Their pertinacity was rewarded and in 1846 the Executive Council recorded a verdict for separation.

However, more delays were on the horizon. Changes in the British Government brought in a new Prime Minister — Lord John Russell — leading a party of colonial reformers. Separation was promised but it was couched in fanciful theories about election and federation. It was only after a great deal of lobbying on the part of the Port Phillip community that separation at last became a reality on 5 August 1850. The Act became law in New South Wales on 13 January 1851 and writs were issued for the first Victorian Legislative Council consisting of 30 men, two-thirds of whom would be elected and the other 10 appointed by the Crown.

The year 1851 was to be a memorable one for the colonists. On 6 February the famous 'Black Thursday' bush fires swept the district. In July, the same month that La Trobe was sworn in as Lieutenant-Governor of the separate colony of Victoria, gold was discovered at Clunes and Warrandyte.

When news of the gold rush near Bathurst in New South Wales had reached Victoria it disrupted the entire community. Labourers left their jobs to head for the gold fields and businesses became depressed. To combat this exodus the Mayor offered a reward to anyone discovering gold within 200 miles (about 320 km) of Melbourne. This resulted in the finds at Clunes and Warrandyte. These were poor, but in August dazzling riches were unearthed at Ballarat and a great rush began with diggers pouring in from all parts of the world.

The pastoralists were dismayed. In 1850 there were 6 000 000 sheep in Victoria and wool and its products earned more than 90 per cent of its total exports. About 50 000 acres (over 20 000 ha) of land were under wheat, hay, oats and potatoes. Shortage of farm labour became chronic as men flocked to the gold fields.

A London *Times* correspondent lamented: 'The flocks of Australia are on the verge of destruction and the import into England of 48 000 000 lb of wool is in the process of being annihilated . . . in my opinion this place is inevitably and irrevocably ruined.' However, wool prices rose to combat the near tragedy of the pastoralists selling out in panic and the miners provided a huge market for meat.

The gold fever continued unabated. 'The gold was all over the bottom like a jeweller's shop,' reported one of the diggers. As more and more fields opened up and yielded rich returns the London *Punch* was moved to comment, 'We have a California all of our own.' Melbourne was soon bursting at the seams. When the first gold was discovered at Clunes the population was 20 000, two years later 600 000 gold seekers had arrived in Victoria and prospectors had spread over the whole north-east corner of the State.

Policing the fields was near impossible. La Trobe introduced a system of 'gentlemen cadets' to collect the digging licences and police the vast areas. The miners' discontentment grew with the increases in licence fees which were introduced by the Government as a revenue booster and to control prospecting. The friction between them and the authorities culminated in the blood-letting at Eureka Stockade in December 1854 when diggers fought soldiers and mounted police.

The rebels were quickly defeated and tried for treason but the weight of public opinion forced an acquittal for them all. After investigations of the causes of the battle at Eureka the Royal Commission presented its findings. It maintained that the diggers 'were exposed to laws unsuited to their natural character' and asserted that the methods used to collect licences produced 'mutual irritation, abuse and gross violence'.

A more enlightened attitude to the administration of the gold fields was brought into being and the provision of generous leaseholds at cheap

Off to Bendigo

The Eureka Stockade, Ballarat

rates was recommended to encourage the miners to have a more settled attitude.

The mining industry began to decline after 1860 and many of the gold seekers stayed on to seek their fortunes in other ways, establishing farms and raising sheep and cattle. Many others retreated to Melbourne and found employment in the urban industries which developed rapidly in the 1870s and 1880s.

In the forty years after the gold rushes social and political development was rapid, and primary and secondary industries consolidated. The 1890s brought a financial crash due to wild land speculation, but the colony soon recovered. Federation was approved, and in May 1901 the first Parliament of the newly created Commonwealth of Australia was opened with due pageantry in the temporary federal capital of Melbourne. The seat of the Federal Government remained here until it moved to Canberra in 1927.

Tasmania

ABEL JANSZOON TASMAN was the first European to sight Tasmania. He made landfall on the west coast in November 1642, in the ships *Zeehaen* and *Heemskirk*. Tasman named the land Van Diemen's Land, in honour of the Governor who had sent him out. He did not realize that he had discovered an island, thinking it was the southern part of the Australian continent. He sailed along Bruny Island and tried to anchor in Adventure Bay but a storm swept him out, and this is how Storm Bay, between Bruny Island and Tasman Peninsula, received its name.

On 3 December Tasman endeavoured to land at a bay on the east coast, and despite the rough weather a carpenter, Jacobsz, swam ashore and planted the Dutch flag. The supposed spot is now marked by an obelisk. Tasman then passed Maria Island, which he named after Governor Van Diemen's daughter. Although he saw no inhabitants, Tasman reported steps cut in trees at a distance of 5 ft (about 1.5 m) from one another and marks of wild beasts feet resembling those of a tiger. He chose to sail away without provoking the wrath of the giants and wild beasts he presumed inhabited this new land.

It was not until 1772 that the island was again visited, this time by a Frenchman, Captain Marion du Fresne. Then followed Furneaux (1773) who had become separated from Cook's expedition. Five years later Captain Cook anchored the *Resolution* at Adventure Bay on Bruny Island. From 1788 onwards, several ships touched at Van Diemen's Land and in 1798 Bass and Flinders circumnavigated the land in a whaleboat thus proving it to be an island.

Landfall had been made by several European explorers, but it was not until 1802 that Britain formally took possession of the island. The numbers of prisoners in New South Wales had greatly increased and it was necessary to establish a new penal colony where the more dangerous convicts could be kept under stricter restraint. The distance of Van Diemen's Land from New South Wales, and its insularity and impenetrable forests, marked it as a place where escape would be impossible. Accordingly, in 1803 Lieutenant Bowen sailed out of Sydney with a party of convicts. He made camp at Risdon, about 2 km from what was to become Hobart.

The following year Lieutenant-Colonel Collins arrived in Van Diemen's Land with two shiploads of convicts and free settlers. The population of Risdon totalled about 100, 22 of whom were troops and about 60 convicts. The only permanent buildings were a few huts and a stone storehouse. Collins quickly realized the inadequacy of Risdon Cove and he decided on a spot about 2 km downstream. He assumed command of the infant colony naming it Hobart Town, in honour of Lord Hobart who was at that time Secretary of State for War and the Colonies.

In the next few weeks progress was rapid. Free settlers were each given 100 acres (about 40 ha) of land about 1 km upstream. A government garden and parade ground were established and work was started on a government farm.

Meanwhile, another settlement was being formed at Port Dalrymple (Tamar Heads) under Lieutenant-Colonel William Paterson. The settlement was named George Town and until 1806 was headquarters for the northern part of the Van Diemen's Land colony.

In 1806, Paterson formed another settlement at the junction of the north and south Esk. He called it Launceston and it became the larger of the two encampments. The two settlements — Collins' and Paterson's — remained independent of each other and there was no means of communication between them except by a tedious coastal voyage.

The settlements slowly grew and prospered until hit by the same famine that was causing such severe hardship in New South Wales. Supply ships only visited sporadically, floods ruined crops in New South Wales and famine set in. In this

192

desperate situation, Collins realized that he would need to turn to the land for sustenance and he organized groups of convicts and settlers into hunting parties which scoured the interior, finding rich supplies of food. Kangaroos, emus and black swans were all consumed with relish.

Thus the settlements struggled along from hand to mouth, occasionally receiving a few provisions from hard-pressed Sydney. The search for sustenance led to the exploration of the interior of Van Diemen's Land. Collins sent an Irishman, Joseph Holt, up the Derwent and he reported that the land bordering the river looked good. Explora-

resettled at Pitt Water (near Hobart Town), New Norfolk in the Derwent Valley, and at Norfolk Plains in the north.

By the time of Collin's death in 1810, supplies had begun to arrive more regularly and deprivations were not as severe. Collins was not replaced until 1813, when Lieutenant-Governor Davey arrived. By this time farming and whaling had brought a certain amount of prosperity to Van Diemen's Land. But the pursuit of agriculture was severely handicapped by the bands of bushrangers who roamed the country slaughtering sheep and cattle and setting fire to homesteads. Groups of

New Norfolk

tion revealed well-watered and good grazing land in the interior of the island and in the Huron River district. Also scores of whales were observed in the estuary of the Derwent.

The early years of settlement and starvation were worsened by the decision in 1805 to move settlers from Norfolk Island to Van Diemen's Land. Most of these settlers, although previously convicts, were now free men. They sorely regretted the move, particularly when confronted with the miserable rations and the fact that they were not allocated convict labour. Many of them exchanged their land holdings for rum, and yet another element of discontent was introduced into the colony. Most of these Norfolk Islanders were

marauders had formed during Collins' time — he had been compelled to release some prisoners during the starvation years — and an ever-increasing number of hardened criminals sent down from Sydney joined the bandits.

Davey was unable to relieve the situation. Denied adequate troops to put a halt to the bushranging he decided on a desperate course of action. In 1815 he proclaimed martial law and imposed a curfew. By these means several bushrangers were caught and publicly hanged. Governor Macquarie in Sydney was totally dismayed by these actions on the grounds that only he had the power to suspend normal law.

Davey was removed and William Sorell took

over the colony. Sorell organized his soldiers to hunt down the more notorious criminals and although the colony was still plagued by criminal activity it was not on the large scale observed during Davey's governorship.

Sorell brought about stricter convict control with the establishment of the Macquarie Harbour penal settlement. The settlement was for the more dangerous convicts and this separation of desperate offenders helped reduce the criminal activity.

In 1815 a new breed of settler began to arrive in Van Diemen's Land. People began to see the colonies as a 'brave new world', a source of wealth and a fresh start. Many of these new immigrants brought capital with them, set themselves up on land and began the breeding of fine-wooled sheep. Sorell showed great interest in pastoral development and imported 300 rams. The industry grew and in 1821 wool was first exported from Van Diemen's Land. A merchant, John Raine, took 65 bales to London. The wool was of poor quality and unsaleable. In 1822 however, a wool trader, Henry Hopkins, set sail for Van Diemen's Land to become Hobart Town's first woolbuyer. He was the first man to handle a profitable transaction — 12 bales bought at 3d a pound in Van Diemen's Land sold in London at 8d a pound.

The foundations of a wool industry had been laid. In the 1820s the island's settlers had bred more sheep than those in New South Wales. By the end of Sorell's term in 1824 there were more than 11 000 settlers and such institutions as the Bank of Van Diemen's Land had been established. The colony had passed beyond the stages of being merely a penal settlement.

Colonel George Arthur succeeded Sorell in 1824, eighteen months before Governor Darling proclaimed Van Diemen's Land a separate colony. Arthur's biggest problem was the reconciliation of the conflicting aims of the settlement; that of providing a strict penal settlement for the transported convicts and that of providing the free settlers with the same rights they enjoyed in England.

Arthur came down hard on the colonist prisoners, but also insisted on a high level of decorum and morality in the new settlers. At this stage about 2000 convicts were transported to Van Diemen's Land a year. Arthur was instructed to punish, reform and distribute these incoming prisoners among the wealthy settlers of the colony. Arthur worked in extremes — he would give con-

victs an early realease for good behaviour or he would severely punish them for a misdemeanour. The very secure penal settlement of Port Arthur was established at this time and along with Macquarie Harbour was used to house the more dangerous convicts.

In 1836, having served an unusually long term and a scrupulously fair one, Arthur was recalled. During his period of office the annual revenue increased sevenfold from £17 000, imports nearly tenfold from £62 000, exports from £15 000 to £312 000. Also the number of churches had increased from 4 to 18, the number of colonial vessels from 1 to 71, and population from 11 000 to 40 000.

Arthur's successor in 1837 was Sir John Franklin, a well-known Arctic explorer. His principal work in Van Diemen's Land was the administration of the convict system but his interests lay in culture, education and religion. In 1837 he introduced a bill that authorized payment for church buildings and the salary of the clergy. In 1839 he founded State primary education establishing schools based on the British and Foreign School Society — a system that had no religious dogma. He did much to foster cultural education in Van Diemen's Land but the incessant opposition he encountered from various council members finally led to his replacement in 1843 by Sir John Eardley-Wilmot.

During Franklin's term the transportation of convicts to New South Wales had ceased and thousands of criminals were being sent to Van Diemen's Land — the only penal colony remaining to the Crown. Wilmot arrived at a period of exceptional difficulty. The free population was demanding a voice in the government of their adopted country and the increasing numbers of prisoners were becoming difficult to control.

The only compensation for the influx of convicts was the material benefit derived from the Imperial funds for the maintenance of the penal establishments. At one time this amounted to nearly £1000 per day. But the Colonial Office cut down on the expenditure and discontent grew. A considerable section of the nominee council were violently opposed to transportation and when the Governor attempted to increase taxation several Council members resigned and Wilmot found it hard to find tractable replacements. He was removed from office long before the usual term

Port Arthur

had expired and died a few days before the arrival of his successor, Sir William Denison.

Denison was the last of the Lieutenant Governors. He held office until 1854. During his whole career he had to contend with bitter opposition. All the wealth and intelligence of the colony outside the official classes was now strongly opposed to transportation and an anti-transportation league was formed. In 1853, Sir John Pakington, the Secretary of the Colonies announced that transportation had ceased.

On the removal of the system which had made the name of Van Diemen's Land odious, the name of the colony was changed to Tasmania and this change was confirmed by Statute in 1855. In that year Sir Henry Young became the first Constitu-

tional Governor of the island. With the new mode of government there began a depression in the commercial affairs of the colony which went on for year after year and it seemed that good times would never return to Tasmania.

Labour was short as a great number of Tasmanians had left to seek their fortunes at the gold fields on the mainland. Farmers and graziers found it increasingly difficult to keep up meat and grain production and the previously high Tasmanian export rate began to decline. Standards of living, prices and wages all fell. The economy remained largely agricultural as there was little incentive to start secondary industries. Political instability was obvious; between 1856 and 1872 there were ten changes of government.

Tasmanian Aborigines

The first inklings of a cure for the lethargy Tasmania was steeped in came in 1871 when a prospector, James Smith, found tin at Mt Bischoff in the north-west. More mineral discoveries followed: a silver-lead mine at Mt Zeehan, gold at Beaconsfield and copper at Mt Lyell. By the late 1870s the mining boom was on. Capital poured in and thriving towns emerged. The population rose to 115 000 in 1881 and to 146 000 in 1891. Export figures soared. Wool, previously the major export, now took fifth place behind copper, fruit, jams and tin.

Tasmania did not escape the general economic depression of the 1890s and one of the major disasters of that time was the failure of the Bank of Van Diemen's Land. However, the continuing mining boom softened the blow.

However it was becoming increasingly clear that Tasmania could not exist in isolation and that her future would always be linked with the mainland. So, in 1899 when the second referendum on federation was held, a majority of almost 95 per cent voted in favour.

The Tasmanian Aborigines

The history of the Tasmanian Aborigines is not a happy one. Shortly after the first settlement had been formed at Risdon, the first of a long series of fatal encounters took place between the white settlers and the Aborigines. This unhappy event which occurred on 3 May 1804 sowed seeds of hostility in the blacks that eventually culminated in the savage murder of settlers and to more savage retaliation.

The affray at Risdon occurred when a party of about 300 Aborigines — men, women and children — was observed driving a flock of kangaroo. The soldiers took this to be a warlike demonstration and, in fear, fired upon them. Thus began the feud.

Over the years the governors did their best to condemn the atrocities but could do little to restrain the savageness and bloodshed. In 1828 the Government offered a reward of £5 for every Aboriginal adult and £2 for every child captured uninjured. Governor Arthur instigated a military operation known as the 'Black Line' in 1830. Five thousand men swept the eastern half of the island intending to drive the natives into a cul-de-sac on Forestier Peninsula. This undertaking cost £30 000 and resulted in the accidental capture of one woman and one boy.

Subsequently, between 1830 and 1834, a poor bricklayer named George Augustus Robinson accepted a Government offer of £100 to look after the Aboriginal interests. With the aid of a few Aboriginal friends he peacefully brought in all but a very few of the natives and settled them on Flinders Island. Despite considerate treatment their numbers gradually dwindled and in 1847 the 44 that remained alive were shifted to Oyster Cove. The last full-blooded Tasmanian Aborigine, Truganini, died in Hobart in 1876.

196

Places of interest

VICTORIA

Melbourne and environs

Air Museum, Moorabbin
Arts Centre of Victoria,
   180 St Kilda Road,
   Melbourne

Botanic Gardens, Royal,
   Birdwood Avenue,
   South Yarra

Captain Cook's Cottage,
   Fitzroy Gardens,
   Melbourne
City Square
'Como' — historic house, Como Avenue,
   South Yarra

Exhibition Building and Gardens,
   Nicholson Street,
   Carlton

Fitzroy Gardens,
   Wellington Parade,
   Melbourne
Flemington Racecourse

Government House,
   St Kilda Road,
   Melbourne

La Trobe Library,
   La Trobe Street,
   Melbourne
La Trobe's Cottage,
   Birdwood Avenue,
   Melbourne

Maritime Museum, Williamstown
Melbourne University,
   Grattan Street,
   Parkville
Mornington Peninsula
Myer Music Bowl,
   Kings Domain,
   Melbourne

National Museum,
   285 Russell Street,
   Melbourne

Olympic Park,
   Melbourne

Parliament House,
   Spring Street,
   Melbourne
Philip Island

'Rippon Lea' — historic house,
   192 Hotham Street,
   Elsternwick

St James Old Cathedral,
   King and Batman Streets,
   West Melbourne
St Patrick's Cathedral,
   Albert Street,
   East Melbourne
St Paul's Cathedral,
   Flinders Lane,
   Melbourne
Shrine of Remembrance,
   Domain,
   St Kilda Road,
   Melbourne
State Library,
   328 Swanston Street,
   Melbourne

Town Hall,
   Swanston Street,
   Melbourne
Treasury Gardens

University of Melbourne,
   Grattan Street,
   Parkville

Zoological Gardens,
   Parkville

Beyond Melbourne

Arthur's Seat

Baw Baw National Park

Cape Schanck Coastal Park
Coal Creek Historical Park
Croajingalong National Park

Dandenong Ranges

Eureka Stockade Park, Ballarat

Falls Creek Ski Village
Fern Tree Gully National Park
Fraser National Park

Gippsland Lakes National Park

Hanging Rock, Mount Macedon
Hattah Lakes National Park
Healesville Wildlife Sanctuary

Kingslake National Park

Lake Eildon
Lake Wendouree
Lind National Park
Little Desert National Park

Mount Buffalo National Park
Mount Buller
Mount Eccles National Park
Mount Hotham
Mount Macedon
Mount Richmond National Park
Murray River Cruises

Ninety Mile Beach

Port Campbell National Park

Sovereign Hill, Ballarat — re-creation of early
    gold-mining town
Swan Hill Pioneer Settlement,
    Swan Hill

Wilson's Promontory National Park
Wineries and vineyards — Geelong-Yarra Valley,
    Goulburn Valley, Great Western,
    Mildura-Robinvale, Rutherglen
Wonderland Range, The Grampians
Wyperfeld National Park

Yallourn Power Station,
    Yallourn

TASMANIA

Hobart and environs

Anglesea Barracks,
    Davey St,
    Hobart

Battery Point
Botanic Gardens,
    Lower Domain Road,
    North Hobart

Cat and Fiddle Arcade,
    Murray to Elizabeth Streets,
    Hobart
Constitution Dock

Government House,
    Lower Domain Road,
    Hobart

Maritime Museum,
    46 Bayfield Street,
    Bellerive
Mount Wellington
Museum and Art Gallery,
    5 Argyle Street,
    Hobart

Parliament House,
    Hobart
Post Office Museum,
    19 Castray Esplanade,
    Hobart

Risdow Cove Historic Site
'Runnymede' — restored colonial house,
    New Town

Salamanca Place,
    Hobart
Shot Tower, Taroona

Tasmanian Maritime Museum,
    46 Bayfield Street,
    Bellerive
Tasmanian Museum and Art Gallery,
    5 Argyle Street,
    Hobart
Town Hall,
    Macquarie Street,
    Hobart

University of Tasmania,
    Churchill Avenue,
    Sandy Bay

Wrest Point Casino,
    410 Sandy Bay Road,
    Sandy Bay

Beyond Hobart

Ben Lomond National Park

Cape Barren Island
Cataract Gorge, Launceston

'Clarendon House' — historic house, near Nile
Copper Mine, Queenstown
Cradle Mountain — Lake St Clair National Park

Derwent River Power Development Scheme — public viewing galleries at power stations at Liapootah, Tarraleah, Tungatinah and Trevallyn
Devil's Gate Dam

Eaglehawk Neck
'Entally House' — colonial restoration, Hadspen

Flinders Island
'Franklin House' — historic house, South Launceston
Frenchman's Cap National Park
Freycinet National Park

Gordon River State Reserve

Hartz Mountains National Park
Huon Valley

King Island

Lake Barrington
Lake Gordon
Lake Pedder
Limestone Caves, Hastings
Longford Wildlife Park

Maria Island National Park
Mersey-Forth Power Scheme Development
Montezuma Falls
Mount Field National Park
Mount Lyell Copper Mine, Queenstown

Old Colony Inn — historic house, New Norfolk

Poatina Underground Power Station
Port Arthur National Park

Queen Victoria Museum and Art Gallery, Wellington Street, Launceston

Richmond — historic village
Rocky Cape National Park
Ross — historic township

Salmon Ponds, New Norfolk
South West National Park
Stanley — historic township

Tasmanian Wildlife Park and Noctarium, near Chudleigh
The Nut — rock outcrop, Stanley
Thermal Pool, Hastings

West Coast Pioneers Memorial Museum, Zeehan

Melbourne city, capital of Victoria, overlooks the Yarra River.
Founded in 1835 By John Batman and John Pascoe Fawkner,
Melbourne has an unruffled style and elegance. (Higgins)

Artist and his wares on a Melbourne city street. (Higgins)

The graceful Flinders Street railway station, Melbourne. (Higgins)

Bourke Street Mall, Melbourne. (Higgins)

The lush, beautifully landscaped Royal Botanic Gardens provide a peaceful retreat for Melbourne city dwellers. (Higgins)

Captain Cook's Cottage — one of Melbourne's most famous landmarks. Brought from Yorkshire, England, the building was erected here in 1934. (Higgins)

Flinders Street Railway Station, Melbourne. (Higgins)

Melbourne's Exhibition Building, built by David Mitchell in 1880. On 3 September 1901 the Australian national flag was flown for the first time, over the dome of this great building. (Higgins)

St Paul's Cathedral, Melbourne. (Higgins)

The shady green banks of the Yarra are a delightful place to relax. (Andrews)

Princes Bridge spans the tree-lined Yarra River, Melbourne. (Higgins)

The Dandenong Ranges, 50 kilometres from Melbourne, are a rare mixture of forests, agricultural and urban environments. (Higgins)

The Great Ocean Road snakes over 300 kilometres from Torquay to Peterborough. Carved into the cliffside as a memorial to those who served Australia during World War I, it is one of the great coastal roads of the world. (Higgins)

THE WRECK OF THE "LOCH ARD"

Shortly after 4.00 a.m. on 1st June, 1878 the 260 ft. long iron-hulled clipper "LOCH ARD", bound from London to Melbourne under the command of Captain George Gibb, struck a reef off the south-eastern tip of Muttonbird Island, approximately 1 km. south of here. Heavy mist had prevented the sighting of the Cape Otway lighthouse. Of the 54 people on board, only two survived — Tom Pearce and Eva Carmichael.

When the ship was wrecked, Tom Pearce, an eighteen year old ships apprentice from Melbourne, was carried out to sea under an upturned lifeboat. At dawn, with the turn of the tide, he was swept into this gorge. Abandoning the lifeboat, he swam ashore, badly cut and bruised. About an hour later he heard cries for help from Eva Carmichael, the eighteen year old daughter of a family of eight immigrants. Eva had been washed into the gorge clinging to a spar which had become jammed on the eastern side of the gorge. Tom swam to her through the heavy surf and floating wreckage and brought her to shore. They both then sheltered in a cave at the western end of the gorge. About noon, Tom climbed the steep cliffs and walked eastwards through the thick scrub until he came upon horse tracks. He followed the tracks until he met two stockmen from the Glenample station, which was 5½ km. east of the gorge.

Hugh Gibson, owner of Glenample, organized Eva's rescue and at Glenample his wife nursed her for six weeks. Although several bodies were seen after the wreck, including one report of eleven in the Blowhole (700 metres west of here), only four were recoverable. They were buried west of the gorge in a site later to become a pioneer cemetery.

Tom Pearce was awarded the Gold Medal of the Humane Society for his bravery and went on to become a ships master. Eva Carmichael returned to Ireland, never afterwards meeting her rescuer. She married C.A. Townshend of County Cork.

DRAWING OF THE "LOCH ARD" DISASTER FROM "THE ILLUSTRATED AUSTRALIAN NEWS", 1878

NATIONAL PARKS SERVICE

Loch Ard Gorge, Port Campbell National Park, was the scene of a dramatic shipwreck over 100 years ago — only two men survived. (Dawes)

The Twelve Apostles — a row of great stone pillars that stand like giant monoliths in the swirling sea at Port Campbell National Park. (Higgins)

Right and overleaf: Port Campbell National Park's greatest feature — the most rugged and dangerous coast-line in Victoria. Over past aeons, the elements have sculpted some of the most unique scenery in the world out of the soft limestone cliffs.

(Higgins)

(Dawes)

(Higgins)

(Dawes)   (Higgins)

Hopkins River boat shed at the flourishing coastal resort of Warrnambool, an Aboriginal word for 'plenty of water'. (Higgins)

Rising in peaks of 1000 metres and encompassing nearly a quarter of a million hectares, the massive sandstone ranges of the Grampians form the western extremity of the Great Dividing Range. (Higgins)

Mackenzie Falls, the Grampians. (Higgins)

The Balconies, the Grampians. Wind and water have eroded many of the sandstone rock formations of these stark ranges into bizarre shapes. (Higgins)

218

Sovereign Hill, a major reconstruction of a gold-mining settlement just outside the centre of Ballarat. (Wigney)

Adjoining the man-made Lake Wendouree at Ballarat are the 40-hectare Botanic Gardens, renowned for their spectacular begonia conservatories. (Wigney)

Floral clock at Ballarat's Botanical Gardens. (Higgins)

Lake Weeroona near Bendigo. (Wigney)

Vibrant garden displays at Castlemaine, an old gold-mining centre situated on the foothills of Mt Alexander. (Wigney)

Maldon — declared by the National Trust to be the 'First Notable Town' in Victoria. The large collection of interesting 19th century buildings and European trees makes this town unique. (Wigney)

Vineyards at Chateau Tahbilk in the Goulburn Valley. (Wigney)

The Mitchelton winery, near Nagambie, was first established in 1969. (Wigney)

Mildura, on the Murray River, was once a busy port with more than 100 vessels passing through in a six-month season. The lock system of the Murray was completed in 1928 and today Mildura is still Australia's paddle steamer capital with restored vessels gracefully plying the river to serve the tourist trade. (Higgins)

223

The grace and dignity of an earlier era is depicted by this elegant band rotunda at Mildura. (Wigney)

Sunset over the Murray River. (Higgins)

Ornate fountain in the heart of Mildura. (Higgins)

The Murray River at Echuca. Situated at the junction of the Murray, Campaspe and Goulburn Rivers, Echuca was once Australia's largest inland port. (Wigney)

Unlike mad dogs and Englishmen, cattle take a break from the midday sun near Swan Hill. (Solness)

The Murray's largest paddle steamer — P.S. Gem — has been preserved at the Swan Hill Pioneer Settlement as a relic of the days when such craft were the main form of transport in the Murray Valley. (Wigney)

Softwood forest west of Wodonga.
The timber is used for the manufacture
of Bryant and May matches. (Solness)

Woolshed Creek at Beechworth was
the site of a rich alluvial gold field
discovered by a local shepherd during
the 1850s. Spectacularly sited on the
edge of the Alps, Beechworth is one of
Victoria's most beautifully preserved
gold towns. (Higgins)

Ned Kelly was once held in this old
gaol at Beechworth. (Higgins)

Beechworth Falls. (Higgins)

The Ovens River flows through Porepunkah, prettily sited at the junction of the Ovens and Buckland Rivers. (Higgins)

The town of Bright lies at the foothills of the Victorian Alps in the heart of the picturesque Ovens Valley. It is an old gold mining town and the remains of the alluvial gold fields can still be seen in the area. (Higgins)

This page and overleaf: Winter months bring snow to Mt Buffalo and skiers flock to the area for downhill and cross-country skiing. In the summer, cascading waterfalls and interesting rock formations are the scenic attractions. Hume and Hovell named the mountain 'Buffalo' as its humped granite mass, rising to almost 1800 metres, reminded them of a bison. (Higgins)

Looking across the township of Mt Beauty, nestling at the foot of
Mt Bogong. The township was created for construction workers
on the State Electricity Commission's Bogong High (Kiewa)
hydro-electricity scheme. (Wigney)

Port Albert, one of the earliest settlements in Victoria, was an established port before Melbourne. Sailing boats once docked here from the United Kingdom, Sydney, America and also China, bringing thousands of Chinese to the gold fields. (Higgins)

Lakes Entrance — home port for a very large fishing fleet — lies at the eastern end of the Gippsland Lakes which form the largest inland network of Waterways in Australia. (Dawes)

Cape Paterson, a popular spear fishing and surfing resort west of Inverloch. (Dawes)

Spectacular rock formation of the Nobbies on the south-western ▷ side of Phillip Island. One of Victoria's most popular holiday resorts, Phillip Island lies across the entrance to Westernport Bay. (Higgins)

Wilsons Promontory National Park — an isolated area of granite headlands, magnificent beaches and thick coastal forest at the southernmost tip of Australia's mainland. (Higgins)

The Hobart waterfront nestles close to the commercial heart of the city. Fishing fleets, scallop boats, trading ketches and visiting yachts find regular shelter at the colourful docks. (Tasmanian Department of Tourism)

Mt Wellington towers 1270 metres over Hobart, capital of Tasmania and Australia's second oldest city. (Higgins)

Wrest Point Casino, Hobart — the South Pacific's centre of glamour and sophistication. (Tasmanian Department of Tourism)

The tortuous coastline on the Tasman Peninsula. (Tasmanian Department of Tourism)

Church at Port Arthur — a penal settlement from 1830 to 1877. Port Arthur is the only substantial convict ruin in Australia and has been preserved as a scenic reserve. (Tasmanian Department of Tourism)

Richmond Bridge, Australia's oldest bridge, crosses the Coal River and forms the main road through the town. The first stone was laid by convicts in 1823 and the bridge was completed in 1825. (Tasmanian Department of Tourism, Solness)

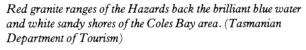

Red granite ranges of the Hazards back the brilliant blue water and white sandy shores of the Coles Bay area. (Tasmanian Department of Tourism)

St Helens on the shores of Georges Bay is the largest town and main fishing port on the east coast of Tasmania. (Tasmanian Department of Tourism)

The baroque fountain was brought to Launceston from Paris in 1859. (Tasmanian Department of Tourism)

Launceston, Tasmania's second city lies in a sheltered valley at the head of the Tamar River. (Tasmanian Department of Tourism)

Devonport, mainly an agricultural city, derives its industrial growth from large scale food processing. (Tasmanian Department of Tourism)

Batman Bridge, at Whirlpool Reach on the Tamar River, is one of Tasmania's most spectacular river crossings. The 'A'-shaped tower rises 91 metres above the river. (Tasmanian Department of Tourism)

The township of Stanley lies at the foot of The Nut — a huge rocky outcrop on the large promontory of Circular Head. (Tasmanian Department of Tourism)

Cradle Mountain at the northern end of the Cradle Mountain – Lake St Clair National Park. (Tasmanian Department of Tourism).

Queenstown, mining centre of one of the world's richest copper lodes, is surrounded by bare scarps dotted with black tree stumps. Sulphur fumes from the Mt Lyell smelters denuded most of the surrounding land in the 1890s. (Tasmanian Department of Tourism)

Water is carried through huge pipelines to the Tarraleah power station below. Most of Tasmania's electricity is generated by water power. (Tasmanian Department of Tourism)

Tasmania's loveliest lake — Lake St Clair. (Tasmanian Department of Tourism)

Lake Pedder, Australia's largest lake, carries 27 times the
volume of water in Sydney Harbour and is 3 times the size of
Lake Eucumbene in the Snowy River Scheme. (Tasmanian
Department of Tourism)

Once a bustling seaport serving the rich mineral fields of Tasmania's west coast, today Strahan's main industry is tourism. (Tasmanian Department of Tourism)

Russell Falls in the Mt Field National Park. (Andrews)

The vehicular ferry returns to Kettering from Bruny Island, historic landing spot of Captain Cook in 1777. (Tasmanian Department of Tourism)

Centrepiece of Frenchmans Cap National Park is the
1443 metre high white quartzite peak. (Andrews)

The Derwent River near New Norfolk. (Tasmanian Department of Tourism)

Tasmania's main pastoral district is the picturesque Midland area between Oatlands and Perth. It is noted for its high quality merino wool and stock raising. (Solness)

A colourful display at the Royal Botanic Gardens set in the Queen's Domain, Hobart. (Andrews)

Ross Bridge, a monument to artistic convict craftsmanship. The three symmetrical arches all bear intricate contemporary patterns of colonial days. (Tasmanian Department of Tourism)

Fern study at the Mt Field National Park — home of a variety of mosses, ferns, lichens and fungi. (Solness)

Suspension Bridge, Cataract Gorge, on the South Esk River. (Andrews)

St Columba Falls. (Andrews)

South Australia and Western Australia

South Australia

IN the seventeenth century the Dutch first sighted South Australia near what is now called Ceduna. The first Englishman to examine these shores was Matthew Flinders who made a survey of the whole of the South Australian coast in 1801 and 1802. Judging from the names he left behind — Anxious Bay, Memory Cove, Mount Misery, Avoid Bay and Cape Catastrophe — he encountered many perils. For many years Kangaroo Island was more frequently visited than the mainland. Whalers and sealers anchored there and South Australia's first white settlers would have been deserters from these vessels who had chosen to stay on the island.

It was not coastal discovery that led to the colonization of South Australia. The area was instead opened up from within when in 1830 Charles Sturt made his great journey down the Murray from its source. Captain Sturt spoke in glowing terms of the picturesque ranges and fertile plains he had seen.

The following year Captain Collet Barker followed up these primary investigations, examined the Port Adelaide inlet and confirmed that there was good land at the river mouth and along the western shore of the gulf.

Meanwhile, in London the Australian colonies were provoking intense interest and excitement. The moving spirit behind the colonization of South Australia was Edward Gibbon Wakefield, an economic philosopher with a questionable private life. Whilst languishing in Newgate prison he developed the theory that the new Australian colonies, such as New South Wales, were experiencing difficulties because the land was so readily available. This, he theorized, led to labour shortages and made the settlement unattractive for capital investment.

Wakefield's theory was that land should only be available to men with capital which would ensure that a certain part of the population would have to remain as labourers for a few years before saving enough to buy farms of their own. The theory attracted a good deal of support. Although the Colonial Office took a bit of persuading, the South Australian Company was eventually formed and the land that Sturt, Barker and Flinders had reported favourably upon was settled.

Administrative control of the new settlement was vested in a Board of Commissioners in London which was responsible for the sale of land and the expenditure of the money raised. Although the colony was founded on Wakefield's principle of sale of land, he maintained that the selling price was fixed too low — Wakefield wanted £2 an acre (0.4 ha), and the Commissioners settled for £1.

However, few people seemed to want to settle in the South Australian wilderness. Those that did buy land were usually investors — absentee landowners who sent their poor relations to manage their holdings. The price of land was lowered to 12/-, and from its very origin South Australia was plagued by the private speculation of officials who had their own money at stake.

Captain John Hindmarsh was appointed Governor of South Australia and Colonel William Light, Surveyor-General with full authority to decide on the location of the capital of the settlement.

Before the new settlers could be despatched from London the Government demanded a preliminary sale of £35 000 worth of land and the raising of a loan of £20 000. In March 1836, eight months after the fulfilment of these guarantees, ships carrying 108 people sailed for South Australia. The *Rapid*, under command of Colonel Light, after sailing up and down two gulfs eventually found the harbour they needed for settlement north of Holdfast Bay. Light described the harbour as 'more extensive, safe and beautiful than we could ever have hoped for'. On 28 December 1836 Hindmarsh, with a party of about 600 people from 4 ships, came ashore at Holdfast

Edward Gibbon Wakefield

(about 55-ha) sections suitable for later division into 80-acre (about 32-ha) sections. His staff was completely inadequate to carry out the farm surveys necessary before sales of agricultural and pastoral land could be conducted.

In the meantime hundreds of settlers were arriving who could find neither land nor employment. In desperation Light sent to Sydney for more surveyors. None were forthcoming so Light then sent letters to the Board of Commissioners requesting more money, men and materials, and the removal of Hindmarsh who was still demanding that the capital be moved. His requests were denied and, deeply disappointed, Light resigned. He stayed on in Adelaide to establish a private surveying firm and died in poverty in 1839.

Hindmarsh was recalled in 1838 and replaced by Colonel George Gawler. Hindmarsh was largely to blame for the delays in surveying Adelaide which in turn led to the lack of agricultural development. But he was more astute when it came to his personal affairs; he left the colony with over £12 000, his profits from land speculation.

On taking office, Gawler immediately poured funds into the survey department ensuring that the immigrants would have land to settle and thus be able to produce food for the community that

The proclamation tree at Glenelg

Bay and proclaimed the colony. The site was fixed and the city of Adelaide founded.

Conflict between Light and Hindmarsh then proceeded to erupt. Hindmarsh insisted that the city was too far (6 miles — almost 10 km) from the harbour, but Light maintained that the good firm land and plentiful water supply from the Torrens made the site extremely viable. While the dispute raged, nearly 1000 settlers impatiently awaited somewhere to live and something to do. On 10 February a public meeting was held and the settlers voted to let Light continue surveying his chosen site. He finished the town survey of 1042 acres by the beginning of March 1837.

His plan — rectangular blocks with open squares and the whole area surrounded by parklands — gave Adelaide a spaciousness and dignity. Light was also instructed to survey the country area for land settlement. He had 59 000 acres (almost 24 000 ha) of land available to the first 400 or so. The lands were to be divided into 134-acre

Adelaide, from the River Torrens

was at that stage relying on food supplies from the other Australian colonies. He employed Charles Sturt as Surveyor-General and Assistant Commissioner in charge of land sales and immigration. Large tracts of country were opened up and land sales were high in London. In 1839 sales totalled £168 462 — the largest sum raised in any one year in the British Colony.

By 1841 the population of South Australia was over 15 000, there was plenty of work available and agriculture at last got underway. Sheep and cattle were overlanded into the area and at the end of 1838 the stock was estimated at 28 000 sheep, 2500 cattle and 480 horses. Whale oil had been the colony's main export but wool soon surpassed it; the value of wool exported in 1841 was £35 486.

Immigrants were pouring in and public services were being provided. Gawler continued to spend money to get the colony on its feet, but in 1840 several things happened to inflict financial difficulties on South Australia. The drought and subsequent failure of crops in New South Wales

occurred. Also inland explorers revealed that the interior of South Australia was an unproductive desert area. Investors in London warily cut down their investments.

Within four years of its foundation South Australia was bankrupt. Wakefield's ideas of land sales and controlled immigration had not been backed by the chartered land company that he had envisaged. From the start the colony had been doomed to run out of funds — particularly with the slow start of surveying the land which meant that people who had bought land in 1835 were not able to put it to use until 1840.

The Board of Commissioners decided that only the British Government could save South Australia and they proceeded to put a halt to Gawler's spending. The British Government decided to take over South Australia and run it the same way as New South Wales, Van Diemen's Land and Western Australia. A new Governor, George Grey, was appointed.

Grey introduced some harsh economies; he cut

wages and discontinued public works and savagely cut the salaries of officials. Emigration to South Australia was suspended for four years and Government expenditure fell drastically. In 1845, a shepherd named Pickett discovered an outcrop of ore at Burra. The only capital invested in this mine was £12 320 and from this, copper to the value of £5 million was taken before the mine ceased to be

there were over 500 000 sheep and 30 000 cattle in the colony. South Australia had become solvent and stable.

Inland South Australia was, however, still unsettled. The pioneers didn't move northwards from Spencer's Gulf, believing that the way was blocked by a great salt and mud flat discovered by explorer Edward John Eyre. During his 1840 jour-

Burra Burra copper mine in 1875

worked in 1877. The discovery of the rich copper deposits at Kapunda and Burra led to South Australia becoming the leading mining colony in the British Empire with mineral exports of £320 624. Excellent harvests produced a wheat crop that was twice that needed by the population. By 1845

ney Eyre had wrongly concluded that Lake Torrens, Lake Blanche and Lake Callabooma were all part of one large tract of water. In 1856 the South Australian Government Assayer, Benjamin Babbage, headed north from Adelaide in search of gold, examined Lake Blanche and realized that it was not linked to Lake Torrens. Several parties were sent to substantiate Babbage's findings but generally the reports were pessimistic concerning the possibility of northern expansion.

More expeditions were to take place and more discoveries made but it was not until the explorer John McDouall Stuart made his overland crossing

Edward John Eyre

from Adelaide to the north coast that the South Australian Government became convinced that the interior was not impenetrable. Stuart found a succession of artesian springs between the northern limit of Lake Torrens and the southern extremity of Lake Eyre. The deposits from these springs formed mounds rising above the level of the surrounding countryside. These enabled him to fix a new base for northern exploration and suggest a more practicable route which he followed.

On 14 April 1860 he sighted what he called 'a most remarkable hill — like a locomotive with a funnel' and named it Chambers Pillar. He was forced back several times by impenetrable scrub and native hostility but in 1862 he at last succeeded and reached the Indian Ocean pronouncing an immense extent of the country he had crossed as the finest he had ever seen. Within a few weeks of Stuart's return land-hungry settlers followed in his tracks with herds of cattle.

The South Australian Government, realizing that there were many large tracts of potentially good grazing country, finally applied to London to annex the Northern Territory. In May 1863 the Imperial Government granted South Australia's request with only one proviso that South Australia was to retain the area only 'until we think fit to

make over the disposition thereof'. A successful settlement was then made at Darwin. South Australia controlled the Northern Territory until 1911 when it became a dependency of the Commonwealth.

There were other ways that South Australia was opened up, the most important of these being the

John McDouall Stuart

use of the rivers. In 1850, envisaging a wealthy river traffic, the South Australian Government offered a bonus of £2000 for each of the first two iron steamers of not less than 40 hp and not exceeding 2 ft (about 0.6 m) in draught which succeeded in navigating the Murray for the 557 miles (about 896 km) from Goolwa to the junction with the Darling. The river presented many hazards; it winded and twisted and was studded with sandbars, and the water depth varied enormously. The two pioneers of the Murray's navigation were an adventurous Scots sailor, Francis Cadell, and a miller, William Randell. The latter, never having

Chambers Pillar

270

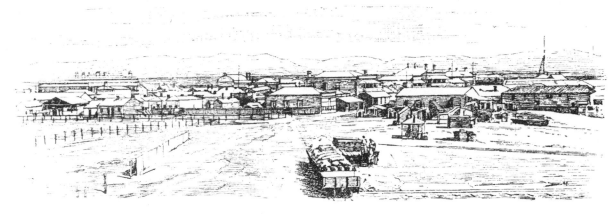

Port Augusta

seen a steam boat before, was the first to build one and sail it on the Murray. The *MaryAnn*, 55 ft (almost 17 m) long, with a 9 ft (almost 3 m) beam, 3 ft (almost 1 m) draught when loaded and a displacement of 20 tons (just over 20 tonnes) was launched at Goolwa in 1853.

However, it was a dry year and Randell's journey was brought to a halt when they struck a sandbar 125 miles (about 200 km) upstream from where Mannum now stands. A few months later he set off again. At the same time Francis Cadell was bringing his 105 ft (about 32 m) long *Lady Augusta* through the Murray mouth to Goolwa. The two steamers caught up with each other near the Murrumbidgee junction, 770 miles (about 1240 km) from the sea. The race was on, the *Lady Augusta* beating the *MaryAnn* to Swan Hill by a few hours. Cadell was awarded £2000; Randall was not as his ship didn't meet the conditions stipulated by the South Australian Goverment. However private citizens awarded another £400. The journey to the Darling junction — a nine week haul by bullock dray — had taken 12 days. The river trade now developed rapidly; properties along the rivers increased in value with the certainty that wool could be moved and stores brought in.

The overland telegraph line from Port Augusta to Port Darwin was the next dramatic event that did even more to open up the central part of Australia. In 1859, South Australian Governor, Sir Richard MacDonnell wrote to the Colonial Office suggesting that the best route for the telegraph would be across central Australia. After much opposition from the other colonies a Bill was passed authorizing a loan of £12 000 for the building of the line. Nearly 3200 km of telegraph line had to be laid over country that was almost unexplored.

After extreme hardships, particularly during the rainy season in the Northern Territory, on 22 August 1872 the cable was joined at Frew's Ponds. In the words of railway engineer, Robert Patterson, 'half of the party seized hold of me and of the wire, and the other half the other end, and stretched with might and main to bring the two ends together. All our force could not do this. I then attached some binding wire to one end. The moment I brought it to the other end the current passed through my body from all the batteries on the line.' Eventually it was connected and Adelaide was in communication with Port Darwin and Europe. The cable also served to open up the surrounding land, giving the explorers a definite starting and finishing point for their expeditions.

The colony continued to flourish and by 1880 nearly half the farming land in all Australia was in South Australia. Drought ruined many farmers in the last half of the nineteenth century but even so by Federation South Australia led Australia in agriculture and was at the same time a substantial wool producer.

Western Australia

THE discovery of Western Australia can conveniently be divided into seven parts. In 1616 the north-western coast was visited by Dirk Hartog in the ship *Endracht*. He named the area the Land of Concord. In 1619 Jan Edels visited Shark's Bay and gave his name to it. In 1622 a Dutch vessel visited the south-western coastal area which was named Cape Leeuwin after the ship. Five years later the portion of the coast lying between Cape Leeuwin and the south-west of South Australia was named Nuyts Land, after a passenger on board the *Gulden Zeepaard*. In 1628 the land to the north of the Land of Concord was named by De Witt and 16 years later Abel Tasman sailed along the north coast of Western Australia and around the Gulf of Carpentaria. About 1644 the name New Holland was adopted for northern and western Australia. In 1697 Vlamingh visited the south-west coast and named the Swan River.

By 1826 both the English and the French had a fair amount of information about the west coast of Australia. The British Government became alarmed by the activities of the French and determined to form a settlement on the western part of the continent. In 1826 Governor Darling dispatched an expedition of 44 convicts and marines under Major Lockyer to form a settlement. They landed at Albany and formally took possession of Western Australia.

The tiny settlement met with formidable difficulties. The land was unsuited to agriculture and the natives were not friendly. However because of the strategic significance of the harbour the settlers perservered.

The following year, Captain James Stirling, also despatched by Darling, explored the Swan River. He journeyed up the river observing 'rich, romantic country', and described the area as 'the most healthy area of the Globe, the degree of heat not oppressive and the nights cool and refreshing'. He strongly recommmended that the area be colonized for 'the French nation have a shadow of a

Major Lockyer

right, founded on discovery, to a portion of the Coast'.

Governor Darling sent his recommendation on to England but it took some time before anything concrete happened. The British Government eventually withdrew their objections and in 1828 they reluctantly agreed to form a settlement at Swan River and sent Captain Charles Fremantle in HMS *Challenger* to take formal possession of the west coast of Australia. A group of capitalists led by Thomas Peel undertook to finance the settlement of 10 000 emigrants. On 18 June 1829 a proclamation taking possession of Western Australia in the name of King George IV was made at what was later to become the township of Fremantle. Parties were sent out to find a good site for a capital city and the site of Perth was declared on 12 August 1829.

The first Governor of the settlement was Stirling who was assisted by a Board of Council and Audit to administer affairs. The land was surveyed quickly. Immigrants attracted by the idea of a settlement free of the stigma of convicts had been arriving with each incoming ship. The British government had promised 40 acres (about 16 ha) of land for every £3 of capital brought into the colony. Unfortunately the 'ideal' free settlement was not as ideal as it appeared. Nearly everyone was a landowner and there were no labourers to carry out the roadmaking and building. The British Government had told tradesmen applying for immigration that there was no need for their services and refused to bring out anyone who could not pay their own fare.

By 1831, 1956 people had arrived in the colony. Settlement began to spread, posing further problems with the lack of communication and roads that were little more than mere tracks in a forest. Thomas Peel proved to be incompetent and was unable even to provide employment for the 300 emigrants he had brought with him. Trial and error changes of the land distribution eventually brought some stabilization.

By 1838 the Swan River settlement was slowly beginning to find its feet. A bank had been established, and 2500 acres (about 1010 ha) were under crop. There was still however, an acute labour shortage and many settlers had either moved on or returned to England. Stirling had even had

enough — he resigned and was replaced by John Hutt.

Hutt tried to increase the productivity of the colony by instigating a rental system of 1/- per acre (0.4 ha) on unimproved property (if it had been settled after 1830) and decreed if it hadn't been improved within ten years the land was to revert to the Crown. The settlers were aggrieved. They had come to Swan River in the first place purely because of the ability to own land and they had endured several years' struggle without enough labour to make improvements on their large landholdings. To make matters worse, the Government raised the price of land to 12/- per acre (0.4 ha) and the sales of Crown land diminished.

In the meantime, a group interested in Western Australia had been formed in London. A company called 'The West Australia Company' was set up to form a settlement under the Wakefield system, whereby land should not be granted but should be sold at a reasonable price.

The company purchased land that had been called Port Leschenault by the French explorers. The settlement was to be called Australind and land was for sale at £1 per acre (0.4 ha) in 100-acre (about 40-ha) sections. The land was surveyed and the *Parkfield* with 93 emigrants under Marshall Clifton (the Chief Commissioner of the scheme)

King George's Sound, from a sketch by Major Lockyer in 1826

embarked from London. After several delays settlement began at Australind in 1841 on Koombana Bay. Two more ships arrived with 400 more immigrants. In the three years between 1841 and 1843, 1387 people, including the Australinds, arrived in Western Australia.

The Australind scheme gave a boost to immigration, but it was to go the same way as Thomas Peel's settlement scheme. The land was poor and the British public lost interest. The settlers drifted away to find better conditions. Timber and coal provided a brief optimism. Jarrah and sandalwood were milled and the West Australian Bank granted assistance to the timber trade. A wave of excitement swept over the settlement when coal was discovered in 1846, however it proved to be of a poor, commercially unusable quality.

Governor Hutt retired in 1846 and he was replaced by Lieutenant-Governor Andrew Clarke. However, he became ill and died seven months later, and was replaced by Captain Charles Fitzgerald. The depressions of the 1840s had not hit Western Australia very severely. However its reputation had suffered because of the complete failure of the land schemes. The colonists believed that the solution lay in more labour and more consideration by the Colonial Office.

After a good deal of argument the colonists came to the conclusion that convict settlement was needed after all. It was felt that the labour the convicts would supply, plus the expenditure of Imperial funds that they would give rise to, would resolve all the settlement's troubles. The British Government agreed and in 1850 transportation of convicts began.

An Order of Council was passed making Swan River a full convict establishment and the first batch of convicts arrived at Fremantle in 1850, 21 years after the colony had originally been founded by free men. The first transportation of convicts arrived before any adequate housing had been constructed. The only jail in the colony had room for 12 miscreants and the convicts spent the first two months aboard their ship. The complete building of the jail took 10 years and it is now the main State prison.

The convicts set to work — roads were made, bridges built, wells sunk and buildings erected. The revenue of the colony nearly doubled in the first years of convict settlement, imports increased and wool became the major export.

Lead and copper had been discovered in the Champion Bay district in 1848 and the Geraldine Mines were established. The surrounding country was explored and found to be a rich pastoral area and the town of Geraldton was laid out. The colony also benefitted indirectly as a result of the convicts. The Home Government agreed to send out free immigrants as well as convicts and over 4000 new free settlers arrived. A military force was stationed in the colony and although a certain amount of lawlessness existed it wasn't as severe as in other penal settlements.

In the words of Mr Sheriff Knight:

The release in this colony of men trained by their prison experience to regard rectitude of conduct as the only sure road to the attainment of success in life has had no contaminating influence on the social condition of the community and hence, after the absorption of so large a proportion of the convict element, the colony enjoys a high state of social order... Great numbers of the convict classes have become holders of property and are thus interested in the observance of law and the preservation of good order.

The convict period in Western Australia was short: from 1850 to 1868 and only 9669 convicts were transported. The roads, bridges and public works are their legacy.

In 1879 the jubilee of the colony was celebrated with the turning of the first sod of the Eastern Railway and the first section of the line was opened up nearly two years later. Towards the close of 1879 the rich pastoral country of the Kimberleys was discovered by Alexander Forrest on his trying expedition across the country from north to east from the De Grey river in the north-west to the Adelaide and Port Darwin telegraph line.

In the 1870s and 1880s the pearling industry established itself on the far north-western coast. Large quantities of pearls were found in the waters of far northern Australia. The most famous, the Southern Cross pearl is regarded as the most remarkable pearl that nature ever fashioned. It is a group of nine pearls in the shape of a crucifix almost 4 cm long. The arms of the cross are formed of one pearl on each side, almost in line with the second pearl. The Southern Cross was found near Broome in 1883 and bought by a London timber merchant for $20 000. Later, English Roman

Catholics purchased it by means of small subscriptions and presented it to the Vatican where it now rests.

However it was the discovery of gold that heralded great times for Western Australia. Gold was discovered in the northern Kimberleys in 1885 and thousands of diggers from eastern Australia and New Zealand flooded into the area. The field proved to yield little alluvial gold, the miners were oppressed by the heat and insects, and many died from scurvy.

Within five years only 300 miners remained in the area. But the gold fever had taken hold and other areas were being searched. In 1887 gold fields were found at Yilgarn and Pilbara, the Ashburton field opened up in 1889, and in 1891 diggers flocked to the Murchison field. Business was booming, deep shaft mines were being set up and miners started moving eastwards from Southern Cross to search for more deposits.

The biggest gold rush in the colony's history was triggered by two miners — Arthur Bayley and William Ford who found more than 100 oz (about 2800 g) in an hour when searching for gold at Coolgardie. Bayley returned to Southern Cross with 554 oz (about 15 700 g) of gold in his saddlebags and the gold rush began in deadly earnest.

Alexander Forrest

Miners flooded into Coolgardie and within a few weeks the ground had yielded 3000 oz (about 85 000 g) of alluvial gold. Gold-hungry men from Europe, America and Africa came to the colony — there was plenty of gold but little water and the Government began boring for it. Afghans and camel trains laden down with water and food were a common sight on the goldfields.

The gold rush intensified in 1893 when an Irishman, Patrick Hannan, reported findings at a field 26 miles (about 42 km) to the north-east of Coolgardie. The field was to be called Kalgoorlie and was known as the Golden Mile. The fabulous Californian and African strikes paled before the glittering brilliance of the Golden Mile, the richest gold area the world has ever known. Twenty years later when the alluvial fields of Western Australia began to peter out more than £155 000 000 worth of gold had been taken from the Golden Mile reef alone.

By 1894 the population of Western Australia had swelled to 81 000. In 1885 when the discovery of gold was in its infancy, there were only 35 000 colonists and 15 000 of these were women.

Living conditions in the fields were rough — flies, heat, dust, the exorbitant prices of food and water (between 1/- and 5/- a gal — about 4.5 L). The only leisure actitivities were drinking and gambling: the average man in the colony drank 25 gal (about 113 L) of beer, a gal (about 4.5 L) of wine or one and a half gal (about 7 L) of spirits each year. But despite the crowded uncomfortable conditions there was little trouble on the fields. Strikes continued to be made and the population continued to swell.

In 1895 the population of Western Australia was 101 000 and nine years later it had reached 239 000. The Government offset the trend of the influx of young male settlers by giving the miners loans to bring their families across from the eastern colonies.

There was an air of general prosperity throughout Western Australia. Water shortages had been relieved by the Government which set up a programme whereby wells were dug and dams and reservoirs built. One of the greatest of all Australian engineering feats was the installation of a water pipeline to Kalgoorlie which helped open up the country between the Avon valley and the eastern gold fields. Rail, telegraph and postal links were established and primary industries flourished with government assistance. Many miners embarked upon market gardening, fruit growing and wheat and dairy farming.

Western Australia did not receive full self-government until 1890 and in 1900 they voted to join the Federation and on 1 January 1901 the new State of Western Australia was proclaimed by Chief Justice Alexander Onslow.

Places of interest

SOUTH AUSTRALIA

Adelaide and environs

Adelaide Hills
Andamooka Opal Mines
Art Gallery of South Australia,
  North Terrace,
  Adelaide
Athelstone Wildflower Garden
Ayers House — historic house,
  288 North Terrace,
  Adelaide

Black Hill Wildflower Garden

Constitutional Museum,
  North Terrace,
  Adelaide

Electrical Transport Museum

Festival Centre,
  King William Road,
  Adelaide
Fort Glanville, Semaphore

Glenelg Beach
Government House,
  North Terrace,
  Adelaide

Historical Museum, South Australian,
  North Terrace,
  Adelaide
Horsnell Gully Conservation Park

Lake Torrens
Light's Vision,
  Montefiore Hill,
  North Adelaide

Morialta Conservation Park
Museum, South Australian,
  North Terrace,
  Adelaide

Parliament House,
  North Terrace,
  Adelaide

Pennington Gardens
St Francis Xavier's Cathedral,
  Wakefield Street,
  Adelaide
St Peter's Cathedral,
  King William Road,
  Adelaide
South Australian Historical Museum,
  North Terrace,
  Adelaide
South Australian Museum,
  North Terrace,
  Adelaide
Sturt's Cottage — historic house

Telecommunications Museum,
  131 King William Street,
  Adelaide
Town Hall,
  King William Street,
  Adelaide

University of Adelaide,
  North Terrace,
  Adelaide

Victoria Square,
  Adelaide

Zoological Gardens,
  Victoria Drive,
  Adelaide

Beyond Adelaide

Alligator Gorge

Barossa Valley
Birdwood Mill Museum
Blue Lakes
Bool Lagoon National Park
Browne Lake

Canundra National Park
Cape Labatt Recreation Park
Cleland Conservation Park
Coober Pedy Opal Mines

Coorong National Park

Dangali Conservation Park

Fleurieu Peninsula
Flinders Chase National Park
Flinders Ranges National Park

Gammon Ranges National Park
Gawler Ranges
Glacier Rock, Inman Valley
Granite Island

Hahndorf Academy Gallery and Museum,
    Hahndorf
Hincks Recreation Park

Innes National Park
Iron Knob Iron Ore Quarries

Jip Jip Conservation Park

Kangaroo Island
Kellidie Bay Park
Koorungle Park Wildlife Reserve

Lake Albert
Lake Alexandria
Lake Eyre
Lake Frome
Lake George
Lake Gilles Recreation Park
Leg of Mutton Lake
Leigh Creek Coal Fields
Lincoln National Park

Marree (Birdsville Track)
Mount Gambier
Mount Lofty
Mount Remarkable National Park
Mount Rescue Conservation Park
Myponga Conservation Park

Naracoorte Caves

Paralana Hot Springs
Pioneer Village, Morphett Vale
Pooginook Conservation Park

Riverland District

St Mary's Peak, Wilpena Pound
Springmount Conservation Park

Valley Lake
Victor Harbour

White's Dam Conservation Park
Wilpena Pound
Wineries and Vineyards — Barossa Valley, Clare
    Valley, Riverland District Southern Vales
Woomera
Whyalla Steel Works

Yatco Lagoon
Yorke Peninsula

WESTERN AUSTRALIA

Perth and Environs

Art Gallery of Western Australia,
    47 James Street,
    Perth

Barracks Arch,
    Perth
Botanic Gardens,
    Lovekin Drive,
    Perth

Concert Hall,
    St George's Terrace,
    Perth

Entertainment Centre,
    Wellington Street,
    Perth

Government House,
    St George's Terrace,
    Perth

Hyde Park

Kings Park

Museum,
    Francis Street,
    Perth
Music Shell,
    Barrack Street,
    Perth

Old Courthouse,
    Barrack Street,
    Perth
Old Gaol,
    Museum Street,
    Perth
Old Mill,
    Mill Point Road,
    South Perth

Parliament House,
    Harvest Terrace,
    Perth

Queens Gardens

St George's Cathedral,
    St George's Terrace
    Perth

St Mary's Cathedral,
  Victoria Square,
  Perth
State Library,
  James Street,
  Perth
Stirling Gardens

Town Hall,
  St George's Terrace,
  Perth

University of Western Australia,
  Mounts Bay Road,
  Crawley

West Australian Museum,
  Francis Street,
  Perth

Zoological Gardens,
  Labouchere Road,
  South Perth

Beyond Perth

Abrolhos Islands
Albany Coastline Reserve
Argyle Downs Homestead — historic house,
  Ord River
Avon Valley National Park

Bay of Isles (Recherche Archipelago)
Beedelup National Park
Benedictine Abbey, New Norcia
Brockman National Park
Broome — former pearling centre

Cape Leeuwin
Cape Leeuwin — Naturaliste National Park
Cape Le Grand National Park
Cape Range National Park
Chichester Range National Park
'China Wall', near Hall's Creek

Darling Range
Dryandra State Forest
Drysdale River National Park

Fitzgerald River National Park
Fortescue Falls
Fremantle: Art Gallery,
            6 Short Street
          Arts Centre,
            1 Finnerty Street
          Gaol
          Kings Square
          Maritime Museum,
            Cliff Street

Markets,
          South Terrace
        Old Customs House
        Prison Museum
        Round House
        St John's Church
        Town Hall,
          William Street
Geike Gorge National Park
'Golden Mile' — Coolgardie/Kalgoorlie/Boulder
  gold mining area
Goldfields, Kalgoorlie
Goldfields Museum, Coolgardie

Hamersley Range
Hamersley Range National Park
Houtman Abrolhos Islands National Park

John Forrest National Park

Kalbarri National Park
Kalgoorlie Goldfields
Kimberley Region
Kwinana Industrial Complex

Lake Argyle

Meekatharra Gold Mine
Millstream Station
Mundaring Weir

Nambung National Park
New Norcia Museum and Art Gallery
Nullarbor Plain

Ord River Irrigation Area
Overseas Telecommunications Commission Base,
  Carnarvon

Pemberton National Park
Pilbara Region
'Pinnacle Desert', Namburg National Park
Porongarup National Park
'Prospect Villa' — historic house,
  Busselton

Recherche Archipelago (Bay of Isles)
Rottnest Island

Scott National Park
Stirling Range National Park
Swan Valley

Timber Museum, Manjimup
Toodyay — historic town
Two People Bay Flora and Fauna Reserve

'Valley of the Giants' — forest near Walpole

Walpole-Nornalup National Park
Warren National Park

278

Wave Rock, near Hyden
Wellington Dam, Collie River Irrigation Scheme
Windjana Gorge
Wineries and vineyards, Swan Valley
Wittenoom Gorge
Wolf Creek Meteorite Crater

'Woodbridge' — historic house,
  Guildford

Yalgorup National Park
Yallengup Caves
Yanchep National Park

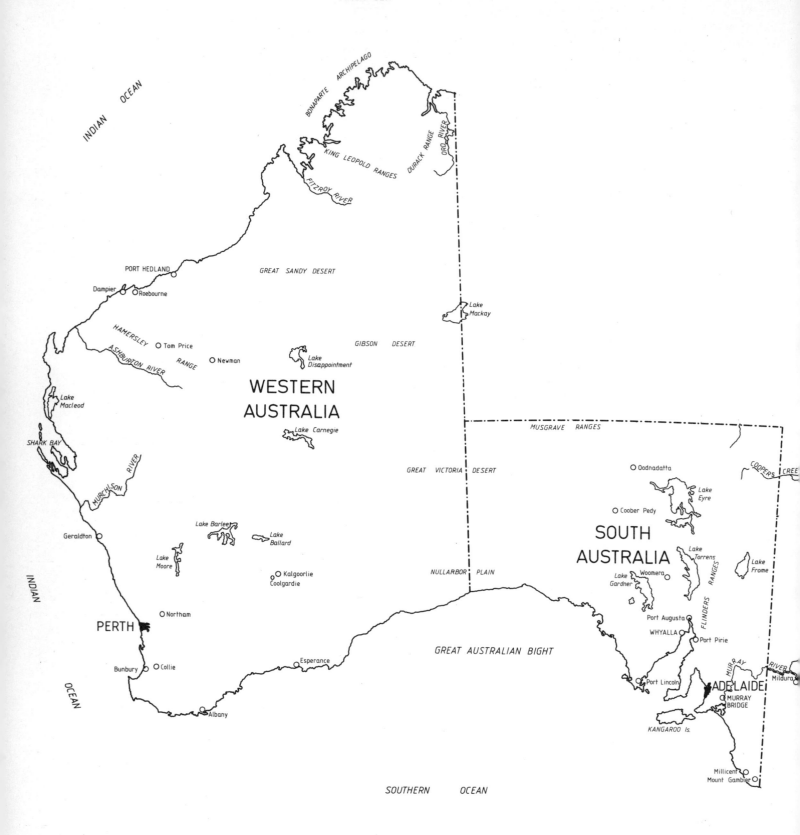

TIMOR SEA

INDIAN OCEAN

BONAPARTE ARCHIPELAGO

KING LEOPOLD RANGES

DURACK RANGE

ORD RIVER

FITZROY RIVER

PORT HEDLAND

Dampier

Roebourne

GREAT SANDY DESERT

Lake Mackay

HAMERSLEY RANGE

ASHBURTON RIVER

Tom Price

Newman

GIBSON DESERT

Lake Disappointment

WESTERN AUSTRALIA

Lake Macleod

Lake Carnegie

SHARK BAY

MURCHISON RIVER

GREAT VICTORIA DESERT

Oodnadatta

Lake Eyre

Coober Pedy

SOUTH AUSTRALIA

COOPERS CREEK

Geraldton

Lake Barlee

Lake Ballard

Lake Torrens

Lake Frome

Lake Moore

MUSGRAVE RANGES

FLINDERS RANGES

INDIAN OCEAN

Kalgoorlie

Coolgardie

Lake Gardner

Woomera

NULLARBOR PLAIN

PERTH

Northam

Port Augusta

WHYALLA

Port Pirie

Bunbury

Collie

Esperance

GREAT AUSTRALIAN BIGHT

Port Lincoln

ADELAIDE

MURRAY RIVER

Mildura

Albany

MURRAY BRIDGE

KANGAROO Is.

Millicent

Mount Gambier

SOUTHERN OCEAN

Spacious and well-planned, the city of Adelaide is situated on the Torrens River between the Gulf of St Vincent and the Mount Lofty Ranges. During the 1880s Adelaide was variously described as 'City of Churches', 'Farinaceous Village' and 'Model City'. (Higgins)

Elder Park, Adelaide. (Dawes)

Adelaide from Victoria Square. (Higgins)

View from Festival Hall, looking towards Parliament House.
(Higgins)

The Adelaide Casino. (Higgins)

Seppeltsfield in the Barossa Valley. Named after the Barossa district of Andalusia, Spain, the valley produces about one quarter of Australia's wines. (Premier's Department, S.A.)

Chateau Yaldara winery at Lyndoch in the Barossa Valley. (Dawes)

Admiralty Arch, on Cape du Couedic, Kangaroo Island.
Pounding seas have slowly eroded the limestone to produce this
spectacular formation. (Dawes)

Still producing fruit after 150 years, this ancient mulberry tree at
Kingscote on Kangaroo Island was the first exotic tree planted
in South Australia. (Dawes)

The Remarkable Rocks, huge boulders poised on a granite dome 80 metres above sea level at Kirkpatrick Point, Kangaroo Island. (Dawes)

Vivid wildflowers throw gnarled vines into stark relief in the wine growing area of Langhorne Creek, South Australia. (Dawes)

'The banks of the channel, with the trees and the rocks, were reflected in the tranquil waters whose surface was unruffled save by the thousands of wild fowl that rose before us . . .' wrote Charles Sturt about the Murray in 1830. (Solness)

Reviving the adventure and romance of the golden riverboat days, the Murray River Queen magestically plies her way along the Murray. (Solness)

Port Adelaide, landlocked and safe, was at its heyday in the 1880s. At that time all letters from Europe were landed here and thence distributed by rail throughout the colonies. (Dawes)

Copper was discovered in 1845 at Burra, and with it came the miners. Accommodation was scarce — many Cornish miners lived like human moles in dugouts along Burra Creek; others enjoyed the relative luxury of the Paxton Square Cottages (right), built by the mining company to improve the lot of its employees. (Dawes)

Vineyards at Clare were first planted in 1848 by two Jesuit priests from Austria. Set in the heart of rich agricultural country, the area is renowned for wine, fruit, honey, barley and wheat. (Premier's Department, S.A.)

Rolling wheatlands in the mid-north of South Australia where agriculture is almost a religion. (Dawes)

St Gabriel's Church, Cradock. This charming old building is no longer used. (Higgins)

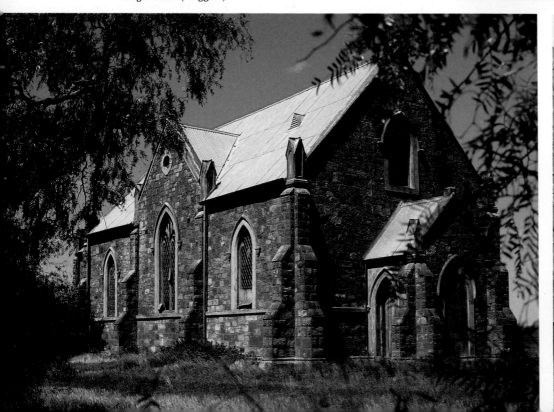

Alligator Gorge in Mt Remarkable National Park. (Solness)

The high cliffs of Brachina Gorge to the north of Wilpena in the Flinders. (Higgins)

One of the most extraordinary geological formations in Australia is the vast natural amphitheatre of Wilpena Pound in the Flinders. The 50 square kilometre park-like plateau is ringed by vividly coloured jagged peaks rising to over 1000 metres. (Higgins)

*The dry stony land of the Flinders ▷
Ranges is rippled with creeks after
heavy rainfall. (Higgins)*

*Overleaf: The Cazneaux Tree at
Wilpena — a favourite haunt of photo-
graphers. Harold Cazneaux, famous
photographer of the Australian pictorial
movement, first photographed this tree
in 1937, calling it 'The Spirit of
Endurance'. (Dawes)*

◁ *Mount Billy Creek at Wilkawillana Gorge in the Flinders Ranges. (Higgins)*

△ *The ghosts of the men who succumbed to the harsh conditions of the outback linger on in this eerie skull-like rock formation overlooking Stubbs Waterhole in the Flinders Ranges. (Dawes)*

Warren Gorge, a popular climbing area near Quorn in the Flinders Ranges. The movie Bitter Springs *was filmed in this area. (Higgins)*
▽

Aroona Valley in the
Flinders Ranges.
(Higgins)

The kangaroo —
Australia's best known
ambassador — almost
camouflaged by vegeta-
tion in the Flinders.
(Solness)

Bunyeroo Valley, north of
Wilpena in the Flinders.
(Higgins)

The old Ghan railway — named after the Afghan camel drivers it replaced — took 47 hours to cover the 1300 kilometres from Adelaide to Alice Springs. The old line was recently closed as it was subject to extensive flooding. (Dawes)

The shores of the Southern Ocean, Coorong National Park. (Higgins)

Shimmering white in the heat — a dry salt pan on the road between William Creek and Lake Eyre. (Solness)

Marla bore — symbol of that precious commodity of the South Australian outback — water. (Solness)

Morialta Falls. (Solness)

▷ *'White fellow's hole in the ground' is the Aboriginal name for Coober Pedy. An appropriate name as temperatures reaching 54°C have persuaded most of the population to live underground for protection against the harsh climatic conditions. (Higgins)*

Opal mining is a multi-million dollar industry which has fostered a spell-binding life style in the South Australian outback. Probably the largest opal in the world was found at Coober Pedy — the Olympic Australis stone. (Higgins)

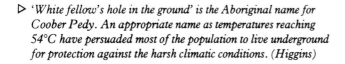

'Noodling' for opal in the waste from the hundreds of shafts which pit the area at Coober Pedy. (Higgins)

'Woodbridge', a historic riverside home at Guildford near Perth. Built in 1885, it is now run by the National Trust. (Higgins)

Perth, capital city of Western Australia, lies on the fertile north banks of the Swan River. It was named and established by Captain James Stirling in 1829. (Western Australian Tourism Commission)

The city of Perth, across the Esplanade parklands. (Western Australian Tourism Commission)

Shopping in Perth. (Western Australian Tourism Commission)

London Court, an Elizabethan-style arcade running from Hay Street Mall to St George's Terrace. (Western Australian Tourism Commission)

The old Court House, Perth. Built in 1836, it is one of Perth's oldest buildings. (Higgins)

The Maritime Museum and Art Centre in Freemantle. (Dawes) ▷

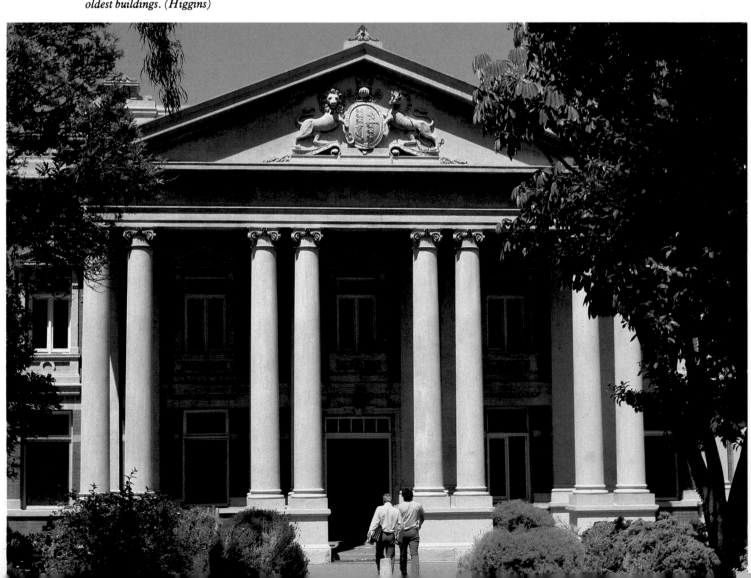

305

Dutch navigator, Willem de Vlamingh named Rottnest ('rat's nest' in Dutch) after seeing many small grey animals scuttling about the undergrowth. The animal, a species of wallaby, is in fact a quokka. (Higgins)

The Round House at Fremantle was built in 1829 and is the oldest building in Western Australia. Originally constructed as a gaol, it is a fine example of colonial Gothic architecture. (Higgins)

Vineyards flourish on the rich loam of the Swan Valley. (Andrews)

A Waugul monolith depicting Cook's voyage, Yanchep. (Dawes)

The huge granite peaks of the Stirling Ranges. In spring the thick undergrowth is tangled with masses of wildflowers — most of them native to Western Australia. (Higgins)

The Pinnacles at Nambung National Park near Perth. These limestone barbs, some standing 6 metres high, rise from a wind-swept stretch of white sand drifts. (Higgins)

Rockbound shores and the lush vegetation of the wind-swept coastline near Albany. The incessant westerly winds sweeping across this south-west corner make it one of the wettest areas of Australia. (Higgins)

Natural Bridge in Albany stands threateningly high above the sea. (Higgins)

Drifting sand is slowly covering the ruins of the old telegraph station at Eucla. Once a vital link in the east-west communications, the station was abandoned when the line was closed down in 1927. (Higgins)

Bold, rocky headlands of the coast near Esperance thrust out into the turbulent Southern Ocean. (Higgins)

A full-scale replica of the brig Amity that brought Major Lockyer and a party of convicts to start the settlement of Albany in 1826. (Higgins)

Naturally sculpted out of granite, Wave Rock, in Hyden, is estimated to be 2700 million years old. This remarkable 15 metre high formation is streaked with water stains varying in colour from deep grey and ochres to reds and a pale sandy tint. (Higgins)

Coastal sand dunes at Eucla. (Higgins)

Beedelup National Park near Pemberton, Western Australia. (Higgins)

Tourist lookout and wishing well on Waverley Heights, Geraldton, Western Australia's second largest port. (Higgins)

Spectacular colour-rippled rock faces border the Murchison River as it twists and bends through virgin bushland of Kalbarri National Park. (Higgins)

The fish are running at Kalbarri, Western Australia. (Andrews)

Vibrant cliff formations of Red Bluff, Kalbarri, form a striking contrast to the blue of the Indian Ocean. (Higgins)

Point Quobba, north of Carnarvon. (Higgins)

Mt Tom Price — 'Mountain of Iron'. (Higgins)

Fortescue Falls in the Hamersley Range. (Higgins)

318

*Folded bands of coloured rock enclose the Circular Pool,
Hamersley Range. (Higgins)*

*Idle asbestos mine at Wittenoom. The town grew up as a
service centre for miners working deposits of blue asbestos in the
Hamersley Range, but in 1966 world demand declined and
the mine closed. (Higgins)*

*Above and overleaf: Rugged landscapes in the Chichester Range
National Park. (Higgins)*

*◁ Crystal clear pools beneath the Fortescue Falls in the Hamersley
Range reflect the golds, greens and pinks of the surrounding
rocks and vegetation. (Higgins)*

Servicing the mineral-rich Pilbara region, Port Hedland handles the largest tonnage of any Australian port and is destined to become one of the greatest iron ore shipping centres in the world. (Higgins)

Built in 1888, the Broome Court House was originally used as a Cable House to hold transmitting equipment for the underwater cable linking Broome to Java. (Higgins)

In the 1900s Broome was a bustling pearling centre with 400 luggers plying the coast in search of the precious gem. Today the heyday is over, but some luggers still fish for young pearl oysters. (Higgins)

'Old Man with Arms Crossed' — a baobab tree on the outskirts of Derby. Having great ability to store water in their trunks, these trees are native to the drought-prone northern areas of Australia. (Dawes)

Geikie Gorge near Fitzroy Crossing, one of the most colourful and spectacular accessible river gorges in north-west Australia. Large permanent waterholes in this area are the home of sharks, saw-fish and freshwater crocodiles. The distinctive change of colour on the rock face marks the high water mark in the wet season. (Higgins)

The 'Wandjina' — one of the great Beings whose staring images are painted on cave walls and rock shelters in the Kimberleys. The Wandjina are important Creation Ancestors of the Kimberley Aboriginal people. (Dawes)

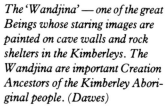

Top left and top right: Windjana Gorge, soaring 90 metres above the riverbed, is one of the most striking features of the Napier Range. (Dawes)

Layered rock formation at Lennards Gorge in the Kimberleys. (Dawes)

The regal, rocky profile of Queen Victoria's Head on the Gibb River Road between Derby and Wyndham. (Dawes)

Waterlilies at Dawn Creek in the West Kimberleys. (Dawes)

Mudflats and mangrove-lined drainage channels stretch out from Five Rivers Lookout at Wyndham, the most northerly port in Western Australia, servicing the Kimberley beef industry. (Higgins)

Ivanhoe Crossing at Kununurra — the Aboriginal word for 'big water'. (Higgins)

Flowers of the kapok tree (Ceiba pentandra) growing alongside the Gibb River Road, the Kimberleys. (Dawes)

Golden nodding sunflowers on the irrigated farmlands of the Ord River Scheme. These were one of the many crops tested for suitability by the Kimberley Research Station, Kununurra. (Dawes)

Rugged, coloured hills surrounding Kununurra — the only town established in the Kimberleys this century. (Dawes)

Ord River Dam, completed in 1972, lies 40 kilometres from Kununurra. Behind the dam lies Lake Argyle, the largest body of stored water in Australia. (Green)

Index

Numerals set in *italics* denote engravings
Numerals set in **bold** denote colour photographs